Wiregrass Country

Folklife in the South Series

Cajun Country
by Barry Jean Ancelet, Jay Edwards,
and Glen Pitre

Kentucky Bluegrass Country
by R. Gerald Alvey

Upper Cumberland Country
by William Lynwood Montell

South Florida Folklife
by Tina Bucuvalas, Peggy A. Bulger,
and Stetson Kennedy

Ozark Country
by W. K. McNeil

Great Smoky Mountains Folklife
by Michael Ann Williams

Carolina Piedmont Country
by John M. Coggeshall

William Lynwood Montell, General Editor, Folklife in the South Series

Wiregrass Country

Jerrilyn McGregory

With Material by
Jerry DeVine, Delma E. Presley,
and Henry Willett

UNIVERSITY PRESS OF MISSISSIPPI *Jackson*

Copyright © 1997 by the University Press of Mississippi
All rights reserved
Manufactured in the United States of America
00 99 98 97 4 3 2 1
The paper in this book meets the guidelines for
permanence and durability of the Committee on
Production Guidelines for Book Longevity of the
Council on Library Resources.

Library of Congress Cataloging-in-Publication Data

McGregory, Jerrilyn.
    Wiregrass country / Jerrilyn McGregory ; with material by Jerry
DeVine, Delma E. Presley, and Henry Willett.
       p. cm. — (Folklife in the South series)
    Includes bibliographical references (p.) and index.
    ISBN 0-87805-925-3 (cloth : alk. paper). — ISBN 0-87805-926-1
(pbk. : alk. paper)
    1. Wiregrass Country (U.S.)—Social life and customs.
2. Folklore—Wiregrass (U.S. : Region) I. Title. II. Series.
F217.W57M38 1997
973—dc20   96-32423
                                        CIP

British Library Cataloging-in-Publication data available

*Dedicated with deepest appreciation
to my parents,
Jerry and Henrietta McGregory,
and to my children,
William, Keith, and Julian*

Folklife, a familiar concept in European scholarship for over a century, is the sum of a community's traditional forms of expression and behavior. It has claimed the attention of American folklorists since the 1950s. Each volume in the Folklife in the South Series focuses on the shared traditions that link people with their past and provide meaning and continuity for them in the present, and sets these traditions in the social contexts in which they flourish. Prepared by recognized scholars in various academic disciplines, these volumes are designed to be read separately. Each contains a vivid description of the traditional cultural elements—ethnic and mainstream, rural and urban—of a geographic area that, in concert with other recognizable southern regions, lend a unique interpretation to the complex social structure of the South.

Wiregrass Country is the first comprehensive survey of a distinctive region of the American South covering portions of Georgia, Alabama, and Florida. Although Wiregrass Country has been customarily associated with poor whites and subsistence existence, this book counters this commonly held assumption with an indepth perspective of the multidimensional aspects of the region. It examines the folk culture of the early Indian, white, and black inhabitants; the development of an economy shaped by agricultural use of fire ecology and later by industries from the north; and the evolution of a contemporary folk culture, rich with music, folktales, festivals, yard art, and outdoor recreation.

William Lynwood Montell
SERIES EDITOR

I am grateful for help from the Department of English at Florida State University, whose endorsement of my research made possible the successful completion of this manuscript. Florida State's support can be measured quantitatively and qualitatively. As a faculty member, I received university support in the form of Black Faculty Support Awards and a Council on Research and Creativity Award as well as departmental funds. While in residence at the University of Georgia, I was awarded similar funding, which initially gave me access to Wiregrass Country.

For their early assistance in directing the course of my activities, I am indebted to Joey Brackner of the Alabama Folk Arts Program, John Johnson and Kem Monk of Agrirama, John Holman of the Landmark Museum, Syd Blackmarr of the Arts Experiment Station at Abraham Baldwin Agricultural College, and Joan Stadsklev of Chipola Junior College. Fellow folklorists Jan Rosenberg, Peggy Bulger, and Caroline St. George helped immensely. I also thank J. Anthony Paredes for redirecting my insights about southeastern Indians. I owe a great debt of gratitude to the series editor, William Lynwood Montell, for his unwavering faith in my work. Others whom I must mention (they will know why) include Roland Freeman, Worth Long, Gerald Davis, Bruce Bickley, and John Roberts.

I received collaborative assistance with chapter 2 from Jerry DeVine. Hank Willett provided the bulk of material on the African American Sacred Harp music tradition in chapter 4. I thank Delma Presley for writing chapter 3, "Rafthands on the Altamaha River." I am also grateful to Beverly Robinson, a member of the four-person team of folklorists who first systematically investigated folklife in the South Central Georgia Wiregrass, for assistance with this book. Special thanks to the American Folklife Center at the Library of Congress, the Georgia History Museum, and the Florida State Archives.

Finally, I am immensely grateful to Wiregrass Country as a whole for sustaining a traditional way of life so that it could unfold ethnographically before my eyes. Special thanks to those who welcomed me into their homes, churches, and workplaces. I have acknowledged most of those I interviewed in the bibliographic notes.

I wish everyone could know Wiregrass Country firsthand. It is a captivating land with a praiseworthy spirit.

Wiregrass Country, a historic region of the South, begins above Savannah and sweeps across rolling meadows into the southwest Georgia coastal plain, fanning over into the southeastern corner of Alabama and dipping down into the northwestern panhandle of Florida. Wiregrass (*Aristida stricta*) depends on fire ecology to germinate. Its fire ecosystem created a unique set of circumstances, tied closely to the development of a way of life. Wiregrass originally covered an area stretching from the Chesapeake Bay to the eastern brim of Texas. All locations, except for the so-called Wiregrass region, acquired subregional names unrelated to the vegetation.

Wiregrass varies in height from one to several feet and is wavy, as its name suggests (see figure 1). Although it was once the most significant associate in a community of species that formed the piney woods, many human inhabitants of the region have lived and died without knowing the plant. Tommie Gabriel, an African American born on a hunting plantation in Thomasville, Georgia, is an exception.

> You were asking about the wiregrass. It's kind of an unusual thing about wire-grass. Normally, you wouldn't see it out there year around. But . . . on the [quail] plantation, especially, we had controlled burning. At certain times of the year, especially, in the early spring, say January and February, something like that when natural foliage died away, then they set it afire out here on these northern places out here. As soon as it burns off, the next thing all the green comes back out. It's amazing how this wiregrass comes up long, thin strands of grass.

For centuries the region of the longleaf pine (*Pinus palestris*) was cotermi-nous with the wiregrass section of the South. Of all the pines, only the longleaf pine can easily endure the sweltering heat of forest fires. The very survival of this "fire climax" species of tree depends on recurrent blazes. It thrives on conflagrations also because they serve to obstruct the growth of competitive trees and shrubs. The longleaf pine takes up to ten years to grow out of the grass stage, during which it resembles wiregrass. A dense layer of expendable needles protects the brushy seedling from combustion.

Smokey the Bear, a very successful fire prevention symbol, has led us to associate all fire with destruction. The Wiregrass ecosystem, however, produces a high incidence of low intensity fires as one of its fundamental

Fig. 1 *Aristida stricta.*
From David Hall,
"Is It Wiregrass?"
Natural Areas Journal
9(1989): 220

natural processes. The region, and the surrounding area, experience more lightning strikes than any other place on earth. This ecosystem thus relies on all the primary forces of nature: fire, air masses, waterways, and topography.

When critical fire conditions are right, each element contributes to a dynamic process. Air masses generate the patterned atmospheric changes necessary for the production of lightning, the primary ignition source. Waterways, which profusely dot the wiregrass landscape with an intricate system of rivers, streams, and creeks, control these conflagrations naturally. The sandy soil ensures that wiregrass is produced for forage and fodder. Because it is highly flammable, wiregrass promotes the spread of fire. Without periodic burning, leaves and litter cast from hardwood trees and shrubs would smother the seedlings.

Wiregrass Country served largely as a hunting preserve for the earliest indigenous population. The southeastern Indians were the first settlers to recognize the ecological benefits of fires caused by man. Seasonally, usually in the spring, they burned shrubs and trees to encourage the growth of herbaceous vegetation such as wiregrass, which they recognized as advantageous to wildlife. Indeed, wiregrass served as forage for the deer population. The lands that were burned were usually those not touched by the natural,

Virgin longleaf pine with a ground cover of wiregrass. Photo courtesy of
Florida State Archive, Tallahassee.

lightning-induced fires. The controlled burns advanced a specific objective
that the southeastern Indians clearly understood.

Fire, moreover, holds a special place in the cosmology of many American
Indians. Southeastern Indians, in particular, consider fire to be the strong-
est entity after the Creator. According to Billy Joe Jackson of the Creek
Nation now in Oklahoma, "Fire is everything. There would be nothing
without it. It is used to grow grass and to get rid of grass. To destroy things
and to help one's self. There's got to be fire." Traditional Creek creation
myths claim that humans descended from the sun. Because fire gave evidence of the Supreme Being, sacred fires always burned in Creek village
squares.

Early white settlers, too, regarded fire as a tool to control their environment. The forest, however, was a potential enemy, concealing social forces
that they judged hostile. The woods were annually torched to "green the
grass," destroy snakes, kill chiggers, ticks, and mosquitoes, and flush out
game. Such burning of the woods took place from 1820 until the mid-
twentieth century. Like the region's original population, the white settlers
virtually made a ritual of burning to enhance their hunting and for full
range improvement.

The white settlers believed that the land available to them for farming

Billy Joe Jackson of the Oklahoma Creek Nation. Photo by Jerrilyn McGregory.

was infertile because it naturally produced little besides wiregrass, pitch pine, and broom pine. Most settlers therefore habitually burned the unfenced forests to maintain their herds. Stock raising and controlled burns went hand in hand. When the forests were burned in the early spring, the new growth of wiregrass was succulent and nutritious for six weeks from March to April. The grass soon became tough, but the livestock would still eat it if nothing else was available. Burning eventually became a custom, something the woods were thought to need every year.

As the following account demonstrates, however, the ecosystem and its people were widely misunderstood. In the 1940s, the U.S. Forest Service appointed a psychologist to determine why the South dominated the national fire statistics. Although informants justified their behavior ecologically and historically, the psychologist insisted that their perpetuation of a "mindless" ritualistic practice reflected superstition. Moreover, he concluded that "the light, sound, and odor of burning woods provide excitement for a people who dwell in an environment of low stimulation and who naturally crave excitement." Ecologically more knowledgeable observers, however, have likened burning to an art. Ed Komarek, who is one of them, commented, "I have spent about half of my life influenced, taught, and educated against fire in nature and then I have spent the other half of it using fire and trying to understand it."

Angus Gholson, amateur botanist, in his herbarium. Photo by Jerrilyn McGregory.

Because of the restrictions imposed on burning, wiregrass no longer thrives as it did in the past. For many years, the so-called experts were the last to understand the role of fire in the evolution and regeneration of the pine forest. They failed to grasp that fire is as important as water in the support of this ecosystem. An estimated 93 million acres of longleaf and wiregrass originally graced the South; today, only 1 million acres remain. The loss may prove devastating, for the Wiregrass ecosystem may be the most diversified on the planet, more so even than the rain forest. At this time, conservationists are struggling to restore the land by respecting its vegetation. According to Angus Gholson, an amateur botanist: "Knowing wiregrass is knowing the history of the Southeastern United States." It is also, as we will see, knowing the folklife of Wiregrass Country.

PART ONE

The Land and Its People

CHAPTER I

Origins

The South has been said to contain more subregions than any other geographical locale in the United States. Many of these subregions have gained wide recognition: the Black Belt, Appalachia, and the Kentucky Bluegrass. In contrast, Wiregrass Country remains essentially obscure. Today, the Piney Woods, the Coastal Plain, and the Pine Barrens have subsumed it. The term "wiregrass" has declined in popular usage. Yet some distinctive characteristics persist and reflect the area's folk cultural inheritance, belying the stereotype of a single southern culture. A folklife study of Wiregrass Country offers a means of reconsidering notions about regionalization.

Wiregrass residents of the past typically found their roles prescribed by the master narrative that is generally accepted as southern history. In part, this narrative describes the South as the land of a few aristocratic whites, a number of poor whites, and lots of enslaved Africans. This characterization fails to do justice to the diversity of the Old South but, with its associated values, helps explain why some residents in recent years have sought to redefine their past in terms of an aristocratic identity.

Those with any knowledge of the cultural area characterize Wiregrass Country as underpopulated, economically poor, and predominantly white. Because of the supposedly poorer quality of its soil and the threat of malaria, settlers did not historically flock to Wiregrass Country, although a number did deliberately settle here. King Cotton played a less pronounced role in the region's early economic development because the soil could not support its production. Most settlers earned their livelihood primarily by grazing cattle and hogs. Most of the inhabitants of Wiregrass Country were poor but proud. For financial and other reasons, these settlers chose the longleaf forest with its inexhaustible range, which precluded dense communities and fostered a particular lifestyle.

The frontier and not the plantation typified the region's developmental history. Slavery, while not practiced universally in the South, produced large plantation systems with their associated lifestyle. By 1860, for Wiregrass Georgia, 22 percent of the landowners had ten or more enslaved Africans. This figure represented a base amount in lower Georgia, but the average slaveownership there had risen from 2.3 to 7.2 in a decade. Even people who did not own slaves often condoned slavery because of their commitment to leisure. Slaves, although they were few, had to perform the more onerous tasks. Many Wiregrass descendants today are proud that their forebears attained prosperity without the benefit of slavery.

Labels like "Poverty Belt" stick to southern states in general. The label "wiregrass" became associated with rural residents with a subsistence lifestyle. The term "cracker" persists and is practically a synonym for Southerners of this socioeconomic background who did not move westward. Ann Malone, one of the few historians to have researched the region thoroughly, has written of a widely held misconception that the forests of the Wiregrass were inhabited only by landless poor whites—backwoods squatters sustained by a few range cattle, hogs, and several acres of stunted corn and sweet potatoes. In reality, by 1850, these yeomen, with their simplified lifestyle, owned the largest farms in lower Georgia and perhaps in Wiregrass Country.

No significant Civil War battles were fought within this vast area. Nonetheless, the people bore hardships. Wiregrass inhabitants of all classes supported secession, and their loss in human lives was tremendous. The Civil War soldiers generally came from the counties with the fewest blacks, the lowest taxes, and the poorest whites. In Alabama, deserters returned to the Wiregrass counties when their families faced destitution. In response, the Confederate troops and home guard inflicted punishment and further suffering. Even Reconstruction affected the region little, since no immediate changes resulted.

Eventually, the region experienced an influx of tenant farmers, African Americans, and northern industrialists. After Reconstruction, African Americans arrived in hopes of becoming landowners themselves, since land was relatively cheap. Employment opportunities in forestry also attracted them. With its virgin forests, Wiregrass Country also held out promise to industrialists. Ironically, with the introduction of guano, a fertilizer, land in Wiregrass Country was suddenly worth more than acres in the Black Belt. Seemingly overnight, the region shifted from a one-crop system to a diversified agriculture with an economy based on naval stores, tobacco, peanuts, melons, vegetables, pecans, and even hay.

In 1860, Wiregrass Country had fewer than six people per square mile, as compared with forty-five in the more economically enriched sections.

By 1890, the lumber and turpentine industries were attracting capital and settlers. The part of Georgia once called the pine barrens and known for bad soil and malaria in the twentieth century became the most prosperous section of the state.

Today "Wiregrass Country" is a name that many lifelong residents of the region have never heard. Regional identity is now subliminal rather than conscious. Over time several factors have probably contributed to the term's decline in everyday usage, especially in Georgia. Some of the larger cities in the South (Macon, Montgomery, Tallahassee, and Savannah) encircle the region. In many respects, Wiregrass Country remains an insular place. Physical isolation has reinforced the reclusive habits of the residents and has shaped the area's indigenous culture. At the turn of the century, few Wiregrass towns had a population of 2,500 or more, enough to qualify as urban under the U.S. Census definition. Urban centers now meet the minimal requirement, and Panama City (nicknamed the Redneck Riviera) is notable among them. The transition from the rural farm to small town life has been accompanied by a lessened awareness of regional identity. Wiregrass was destroyed by the settlers who cultivated the land and vanished from the minds of urban dwellers who migrated from the farms.

Some residents now identify with their region through popular culture. Residents of the Alabama Wiregrass hear the term used by local media, businesses, and social organizations. The largest regional newspaper—the *Dothan Eagle*—and local television networks call Dothan, Alabama, the "Hub of the Wiregrass." Consequently, residents in the tristate area nearest to Dothan personally identify with wiregrass but only as a nickname. In Enterprise, Alabama, for example, about thirteen establishments use the word in their names. In Alabama, a hospital, a masonic lodge, and a museum all do so.

Wiregrass Georgia has no metropolitan zones comparable to Dothan. Dothan, Alabama, has a population of 54,000, up from 60 in 1888, and was once described as a small town on the site of a cowpen. Cities in Wiregrass Georgia lack Dothan's present infrastructure and a sense of wiregrass as a cultural marker. The local media are few and small.

Wiregrass soil initially shaped the region's negative self-image. The terms "piney waste" and "wiregrass" were originally interchangeable and had derogatory connotations. Where "wiregrass" bore a derogatory meaning, connoting poverty and ignorance, residents learned to shun any affiliation with it. Alabama countered the negative image, which took its toll on the psyche of the residents, by defiantly billing Dothan as the "Queen City of the Wiregrass." Positive associations with the region will presumably also be reinforced by signs for Highway 84, which dissects lower Georgia and was recently designated "Wiregrass Georgia Parkway."

The Wiregrass Documentary Project, of which the present book forms part, sought primarily to complete ethnographic research on the folklife of one of the South's more neglected cultural regions. Wiregrass Country retains many of its rural characteristics. It has few malls of even the strip variety. Large water towers are more ubiquitous than stately courthouses or city halls. The railroad industry created many small towns separated by only seven miles or so, in accordance with railroad policy on the distance between stations. The railroad era contributed to the region's rich cultural heritage.

This first full portrait of Wiregrass Country aims to increase general awareness and understanding of historical and contemporary folklife traditions in the region. Although theoretical research in folklore has expanded, folklife remains a neglected area. Folklife traditions from regions like the Wiregrass in particular remain largely unrecognized and untapped. In theory, folklore embraces myth, legends, folktales, jokes, proverbs, riddles, and other genres and subsumes folklife, which denotes research into everyday traditions. In practice, however, the term's usage differs. While in many European countries, folklife means the study of everyday traditions, in the United States it usually means only material culture. Impetus has been lacking to study the total range of folk cultural phenomena. Yet knowledge of the subfield is necessary for the fruitful study of regional culture.

From the beginning, I decided to take an ethnographic approach and to draw on structured observation. It was insufficient to rely on informants' reports, because local residents often regard folk cultural traditions, which are familiar from everyday use, as insignificant and consequently overlook them. My goal, then, was to provide an in-depth comparative analysis of social life as it had evolved within this region.

Through formal interviews, I recorded life histories so that I could interpret them and reconstruct the cultural past and compare contemporary folklife traditions with it. Initially I veered away from the "authoritative" civic community and concentrated on documenting the processual unfolding of public display events and cultural performances over time. I then backed up certain observations through oral historical accounts. I recruited informants through chance encounters, official referrals, and word of mouth.

I had great difficulty with one threshold question. Where do Wiregrass Country's boundaries lie? Past studies furnished no guidance. On the one hand, areas of the South in which the plant once grew abundantly did not all share the same historical and cultural features. If I relied on the area associated with the term in popular usage, as did geographer Mary Hale, only the Alabama Wiregrass would qualify. Unfortunately, Hale took her cues from formal institutions such as postmasters, agricultural agents, and newspaper editors.

Nor is any consensus as to the region's boundaries evident in available maps by geographers, historians, and botanists. Disuse of the word "wiregrass," a shift in economic factors, and the defoliation of wiregrass's physical habitats have undermined past efforts at definition. The area's boundaries inevitably overlap and blur. Certainly cultural and social ties (including kinship) within the region have shown little regard for state boundaries. Commercial and political bonds have followed suit. There is greater agreement among the residents, especially where about half a dozen Florida and Alabama counties are concerned.

Nonetheless, vegetation and cultural and social history offer some helpful clues. On the one hand, despite many shared physical characteristics, Thomasville, to the north of Tallahassee, Florida, appears to lie within the region. Here state boundaries are closely aligned with vegetational growth. On the other hand, Tallahassee, labeled "Piedmont Florida" akin to the "Red Hills of Georgia," may be placed on the fringe of Wiregrass Country.

The longleaf pine, and by inference its associate, wiregrass, rarely appear within Tallahassee because heavy cultivation dating back to the American Indians has caused hardwood trees to replace the stately pine. The Tallahassee region—longer and more extensively cultivated than any other area of the same size in Florida—was abandoned after being home to generations of American Indians. Moreover, Tallahassee's cultural development differed from that of other Wiregrass communities. In 1850, the county possessed three times as many planters as did Wiregrass counties. Nearby Calhoun County, Florida, for example, had only two planters.

Anomalies did exist within the historic Wiregrass. Large plantations resembling Black Belt communities sprang up in strategic places. Thomas County in Georgia, Barbour County in Alabama, and Jackson County in Florida are several of the historic Wiregrass counties in which a plantation tradition coexisted with subsistence farming. Landowners located near fertile river outlets generally had a better means of getting their cotton to the market. Such an advantage created pockets of elegance and luxury in the midst of hardship and provincialism. The aristocratic minority lived in a socially limited and closed world.

In defining the region, then, I have relied on the county historians and vernacular mappings, following the lead of some popular and scholarly writers before me. These sources often proved vital in determining the outer limits. Inevitably, the phrase "Wiregrass Country" is historical, denoting a region of the South and specific to the past of that region. To establish the borders now entails a twentieth-century judgment of the ways in which nineteenth-century people defined themselves. It is also impor-

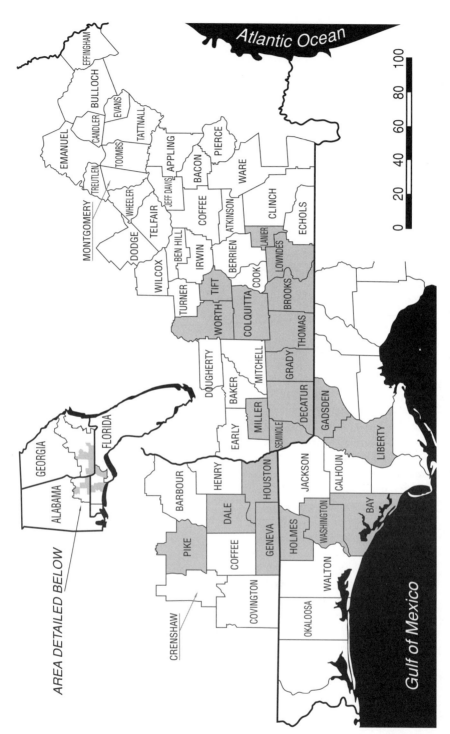

Fig. 2 Map of Wiregrass Country and surrounding counties.

tant to bear in mind that cultural domains, far from being stationary, are constantly shifting and mutable.

The shaded area in figure 2 indicates the main subregion that I covered. Its extent was of course limited by the available time, energy, and money. For the sake of cost effectiveness, I had to take into account the time expended just driving between points. Despite the geographically restricted focus of my work, few counties in the region altogether escaped my attention.

No comprehensive studies of Wiregrass Country presently exist, and no regional historians or folklorists recorded the folklife of the total cultural area. On the whole, the region is still neglected by writers. In the words of Minnie Boyd, the historian, it has "long histories of sturdy yeomen awaiting their scribes." My written sources, then, included county histories, dissertations, and local color writers. I found few travel accounts. Trips into Wiregrass Country were apparently infrequent or did not inspire much documentation.

Chipola Junior College in Marianna, Florida, has the field notes from the Southern Arts Federation's Rural and Minority Arts Initiative, and some other helpful reports exist. In 1977, the American Folklife Center conducted a field survey in eight counties of Wiregrass Georgia under the auspices of the Arts Experiment Station at Abraham Baldwin Agricultural College. Over the course of the summer months, four full-time folklorists investigated South Central Georgia extensively and eventually produced an exhibit and a publication. These documents guided the present documentary project, but I did not retrace the same ground. Although the eight counties surveyed perhaps represent the heart of Wiregrass Georgia, I treat the tristate area with Dothan, Alabama, at its center.

Another regional institution of some note is Agrirama, a living history museum in Tifton, Georgia. In 1981, it commissioned several significant but unpublished reports as part of its Wiregrass Rural History Research Project. The key contributors were Ann Malone and Jerry DeVine, who wrote on such subjects as recreation in South Central Georgia from 1870 to 1900, the turpentine industry, livestocks and poultry, and major crops and their culture. The Landmark Museum in Dothan, Alabama, and the Pike Pioneer Museum in Troy, Alabama, daily showcase a historical reconstruction of regional folklife. Such outdoor museums may be revivalistic in approach, yet as archives they have some value for researchers. Several dissertations treat aspects of Wiregrass folklore and folklife and give this book an interdisciplinary thrust. The authors should be commended for their attention to genres such as folktales, songs, and occupational and religious folklore.

Other southern regions have perhaps developed more famous local color writers. Unlike other available evidence about the region, however, journalistic accounts are relatively plentiful. Wiregrass Country once had a plethora of newspapers. Several produced columnists who wrote about the locale's cultural, historical, and social past. E. W. Carswell, one contemporary example, has been quite prolific. Carswell, a Florida Heritage Award winner, conscientiously promotes understanding of folklife in the region in hopes of helping preserve some of its customs and folkways. For years his column appeared in the *Pensacola Journal* every week.

The county histories are very interesting and irregular but plentiful. Many counties within Wiregrass Country are the youngest in their states. Houston County in Alabama, Grady County in Georgia, and Bay County in Florida were created in this century from previously existing counties. Some local historians wrote several accounts of their own counties and adjacent ones. Genealogical materials found in county libraries sometimes afford insights regarding folklife within their area. For the most part the documentation of folklife is scant, however, and many Wiregrass counties still await their historians.

Although many contemporary residents are unconscious of any regional identity, Wiregrass Country nevertheless has a cultural unity. As the following pages indicate, residents of the tristate region tend to be communal, frugal, and hardworking. The patterned social interactions of today attest to the region's unique cultural inheritance. Part 1 considers the diverse immigrants who attempted to create a homeplace within Wiregrass Country. Part 2 surveys the region's characteristic musical and verbal art traditions. Part 3 investigates regional forms of entertainment and recreation.

CHAPTER 2

Indians, Settlers, and Slaves

The residents of Wiregrass Country included American Indians, Europeans, and Africans. Alliances developed among them for self-preservation and to protect their interests. Individual lives intersected economically, politically, and culturally in ways peculiar to the region, especially in relation to slavery, trade, and acculturation.

From ancient times, Wiregrass Country offered a home to many diverse groups. The area's first population came in successive waves from the Northwest, pursuing large animals such as mastodons and the ground sloth. Few specific ancestral links can be shown to have existed between these Paleo-Indians and the aboriginal population that first encountered Europeans in the region. The settlers generally found Wiregrass soil problematic for cultivation because it was easily made barren. In consequence, little archaeological evidence of permanent occupancy survives in the Wiregrass except, significantly, along some of its fertile riverbanks. Communal farming developed for the cultivation of staple crops such as corn and beans, which tended to exhaust the soil quickly.

Much of Wiregrass Country served as an extensive hunting preserve with an abundance of wild game. Early indigenous societies survived by subsistence farming and hunting. The men often traveled great distances from their settlements in the search for deer, bear, turkey, rabbit, squirrel, and other animals. Hunters' trails provided the original routes for many of our current highways.

Wiregrass Country affords some archaeological evidence of the Gulf culture, which developed by about A.D. 1000. These Indians founded towns built around massive, flat-topped earthen pyramids that served as spectacular ceremonial foundations for their religious temples and sometimes held the burial crypts of high-ranking individuals. The Gulf cultural influence apparently spread into present-day Early County, Georgia, near the Chattahoochee River. Nine massive mounds were built upon the Kolomoki site during the twelfth and thirteenth centuries. The Temple Mound, which is fifty-six feet high, is the most impressive and stood at the religious center of the village. Another mound nearby was evidently used for important ball games. The builders disappeared 900 years ago for reasons unknown.

During the period leading up to European exploration and settlement, the region's inhabitants included the Apalachicola, Apalachee, and Chatot peoples. These ancestors of the Indians who were later removed to the Western Territory had evolved agrarian societies and differed greatly from the hunter-gatherers who preceded them. They formed towns and villages and developed a sense of community. The many clans of the southeastern Indians served as central units of social organization falling between the nuclear family and the political territories. Clan membership provided a central identity that predetermined marital, political, and ceremonial obligations. Clan names—bear, deer, panther, alligator, and wind—reflected associations with animals or natural phenomena.

Individuals lived mainly in a town (*talwa* in Creek), the seat of political and ceremonial life, which revolved around a square area or ceremonial plaza. Here elders and idlers congregated and all business transactions took place. The talwa was the site of the Busk, or Green Corn, Ceremony, an annual celebration with great ritual significance. The festival occurred in the great house of the public square. It marked a new year, a time for atonement and personal renewal. To commemorate this occasion, women broke and replaced all of the household utensils that they had used for the past year. Men refurbished all of their property so that it looked new. No one was supposed to eat any of the new corn before the annual busk. The ceremony itself lasted eight days and was solemnized by the lighting of a new town fire. Each woman then took an ember home so that she could start a new fire on the family hearth.

A village (*huti*) was a satellite of the square town and was often connected to it by footpaths. The villages, small matrilocal communities, were situated near rivers and springs. They were probably confined to the water's edge so that corn could be grown without fertilizer. The cultivation of crops was a job primarily for women, who were wise enough not to waste their labor on unproductive soil. Before planting seeds, the women pierced the ground with pointed sticks. Beans and corn usually grew together in the same field. The cornstalks acted as a natural support for the sprouting beans. A huti was abandoned when the land became infertile. Its residents shifted their communal plantation elsewhere.

By 1540 the first European explorers had arrived in Wiregrass Country.

The region was one of the first in North America north of Mexico to experience foreign invasion. *Conquistador*—"conqueror"—aptly describes the Spanish presence in this part of the world. Hernando de Soto assembled a virtual armada of ships and men to conquer North America's Indians. His fleet of nine vessels sailed from Havana with an army of about 600 men and perhaps 100 more camp followers and servants. Also on board were more than 200 horses, a herd of hogs, some mules, dogs to track the Indians, and all the food and equipment believed necessary to outfit the army and start a colony. Once in Florida, de Soto marched through the heart of Wiregrass Country. He had been designated governor of Cuba and Florida by the king of Spain, and he evidently took the position seriously. Regardless of the reception given him and his men, he left behind him death and destruction. His army and its followers raided storehouses, squandered food, and plundered villages looking for treasures.

Until about 1759, most of Wiregrass Country was nominally Spanish. The Spanish sphere of influence extended into the Georgia Wiregrass from Florida. The Spanish mission system took a terrible toll in lives. Immediately following the introduction of European civilization, the aboriginal population dropped abruptly as a result of European diseases, to which the Indians had no immunity; competition among the Indians for benefits from the Spaniards; and punitive actions by the conquerors. The Spanish Empire expected to win allegiance and obedience by converting the indigenous population to the Roman Catholic faith. Groups that assented to conversion, such as the Timucuans, often did not survive. Christened at the start of the seventeenth century, many Indian peoples soon found themselves doomed to disease and exploitation, including attacks by raiders from the Carolinas in pursuit of fugitive slaves. Remnants of tribes that survived contact with the Spanish in Wiregrass Country would later comprise the Creek Nation.

As colonization destroyed the earlier population, Wiregrass Country became more and more the political domain of the Muskogees. "Muskogee" is the name generally assigned to most of the indigenous ethnic groups in the area after contact with the Europeans. In time the Muskogees and affiliated groups united to form the Creek Confederacy. Although Anglo Americans designated them part of the Five Civilized Tribes—Cherokee, Chicksaw, Choctaw, Creek, and Seminole—in reality the Confederacy consisted of innumerable unaffiliated survivors. As this description indicates, the Creeks were an ethnically diverse group. The names of American Indian groups, typically bestowed upon them by their neighbors, often reflected their particular languages. Ironically, however, the Creeks were named for their habitation patterns as perceived by white settlers.

In the eighteenth century, the English, Spanish, and Creek populations fought over their claims to much of the Wiregrass region. In the process English raiders virtually exterminated the original peoples, especially in Florida. In 1704, for example, Colonel James Moore of South Carolina invaded the area and destroyed many Spanish missions. His forces enslaved, sold, and shipped to the West Indies an incalculable number of captives. At Moore's hands, the Apalachee became the first group with Wiregrass affiliations to be practically annihilated. The remnants moved west to Louisiana and in some cases eventually to northern Mexico. Florida was to be virtually emptied of its aboriginal population.

Along with their system of government and religion, Europeans brought their brand of trade to the aboriginal peoples. The traders used articles of European manufacture to promote dependency among the Indians and to subdue them. Items used as trade goods or gifts to the southeastern Indians included tools, glass beads, small bells, flour, firearms, and cloth. Seduced by such products, the Creek Confederacy eventually turned to commercial hunting, which changed their way of life.

The English traders divided the Creek Confederacy further into two geographical groups called the Lower and Upper Creeks. There were differences between these subdivisions, but they both exhibited the same cultural patterns. Most of the Lower Creeks, for instance, spoke Hitchiti, a Creek dialect related to the Muskogee language of the Upper Creeks. At one time Hitchiti speakers were probably the most important group in southern Georgia and their language probably the most widespread. The Lower Creeks are considered to have founded the Creek towns within a certain part of the Wiregrass. The Upper Creeks, on the other hand, occupied a different trade route farther north where the Coastal Plain joins the Piedmont.

The dominant characteristics of the Creek Nation were destined to change as a new force emerged to seal their fate. The offspring of intermarriages, which were pervasive, were a more acculturated people thoroughly familiar with European customs and values. They often assumed leadership positions within a matrilineal society. Although they remained full-fledged members of the Creek Nation, they bore names such as McGillivray, Weatherford, and McIntosh. These acculturated Indians, moreover, negotiated many of the treaties that led to removal. With a few exceptions like William Weatherford, most tended to support the political agendas of their white fathers. Many treaties and trade agreements came into being because of such ties. William McIntosh and others like him generally supported an agrarian economy and Western cultural and political hegemony as a way of gaining "respectability." McIntosh has been described as the best-known Creek in the United States, someone acquainted with the Southeast's political and military leaders, and a favorite among those who recommended "civilizing" the Indians.

A conflict eventually developed between the various factions, which escalated into a form of civil war. In the Creek War of 1813–1814, the different government-backed factions fought each other. Perceiving the Upper Creeks to be unduly hostile and restless, the U.S. government decided to intervene and sent an invading army to restore "proper" order. Future president Andrew Jackson gained much of his fame when he commanded the American armed forces with a prominent band of Lower Creek allies. This conflict became known as the Red Stick War.

Traditionally, the Creek Nation had a moiety system, which divided their society into two groups, the red and the white. Clans responsible for declaring war lived in red towns, and those responsible for negotiating peace lived in white ones. At one time, the white clans probably possessed the greater prestige, being able to offer sanctuary and friendship to refugees. As a result of colonization, the war clans began to retain clout during peaceful times, causing the white clan members to become trade brokers and allies with Americans to retain influence. After their defeat during the Creek War, many of the hostile Creeks sought refuge in Spanish territory across the Florida border among the Seminoles and African maroons, creating a powerful alliance.

Between 1740 and 1812, the expanding Anglo settlements in Alabama and Georgia put pressure on many Creeks, especially the Seminoles, to enter Spanish Florida and establish fortifications. The *Siminoli* ("wild" or "exiles," depending on the translator) drifted from the Creek Nation in 1750 and emigrated into Florida. Once there, they merged with remnants of the earlier population. From this beginning, the Seminole people's experiences diverged from those of the other southern Indian groups. Whereas other groups diminished with European contact, the Seminoles grew incrementally as the dissident Creeks joined them.

As the Seminoles were arriving in Florida, African maroons were emigrating into North Florida. American Indians, Europeans, and Africans met and mingled more in Florida and the colonial Southeast generally than anywhere else in the United States. The Spaniards regularly granted asylum to any fugitives who would convert to Catholicism, and many of them did so. As early as 1738, enslaved Africans began escaping from South Carolina to take refuge in what was then Spanish territory. After the War of 1812, as a departing gesture, the British relinquished their fort on the Apalachicola River to their Creek, Seminole, and African allies. This stronghold became known as the Negro Fort because about 300 refugee African maroons occupied it, with perhaps another 1,000 settled nearby. In 1816, gunboats attacked the fort, setting off an ammunition room and killing several hundred fugitive slaves. Those who did not escape to other villages and were not massacred were reenslaved.

The escaped Africans and the Seminoles continued to work together, so much so that the Seminoles were described as having evolved into a nation practically controlled by Africans. The Africans played a crucial role as interpreters and intelligence agents. Being more knowledgeable about the semitropical terrain, certain agricultural skills, Europeans and their culture, and European languages, the Africans attained some primary positions of leadership among the newcomers. In so doing, the Africans moved freely among the different cultures, at various times interpreting Creek to Creek, Creek to Europeans, and white men to Creek.

Although the Seminoles practiced slavery, the Africans among them were not slaves in the usual sense of the word and were regarded in most cases as equals. Enslaved Africans could build their own farms and paid a moderate rent to their Indian masters. The resulting vassalage was somewhat democratic and apparently devoid of racial oppression. The Seminoles had a history of adopting outsiders, and the Africans were considered no exception to this tradition. In exchange, the Seminoles learned how to survive in a semitropical climate. Dryland rice cultivation may have been one of the agricultural skills that Africans taught the Indians. Despite this cultural exchange, there was some friction between the two groups, and it was exacerbated by the settlers.

The white settlers' approach to the Indians differed only in degree from that taken by the Spanish. As soil became depleted in Virginia and the Carolinas, residents of these states commonly penetrated the lower South and eventually entered Wiregrass Country. By 1821, the Spaniards had ceded Florida, and the area was open for American settlement. Before the Spanish land cession, during both the Revolutionary War and the War of 1812, the British had formed alliances with the Creeks against the American forces. After the American victories, the fledgling federal government found itself too weak to subjugate the indigenous population and instead resorted to deceit in the form of trade and treaties. In some instances, government-sponsored trading posts were established all along the frontier, and credit was liberally extended to individual Indians. When Indians lacked specie to pay their debts, government agents took land instead. The federal government in this way would deliberately defraud the American Indians and strip them of their property.

Although the British were now gone, the Americans remained constantly at war with the Creeks, Seminoles, and African maroons. After a lottery in Wiregrass Georgia, white settlers immediately began to acquire land. According to the terms of the lottery, all free white men who were twenty-one, a U.S. citizen, and a resident of the state were entitled to par-

Ben Bruno, interpreter for
the Seminoles. Photo
courtesy of the Florida
State Archive, Tallahassee.

ticipate in the drawing. The fortunate ones were dispersed throughout
Georgia. Other individuals had received Bounty Land Warrants for their
service in the Revolutionary War and the War of 1812. The desire for land
resulted in continual agitation for the removal of the southeastern Indians.

By the Treaty of Fort Jackson, which was intended to relieve the tension,
Americans forced even their Lower Creek allies to cede nearly two-thirds
of their land. This treaty led to the opening of much of the Wiregrass
for settlement. Men like William Hawthorne of North Carolina came to
Wiregrass Country leaving behind soil that had already been depleted, and
he led others to the area, which he described as a garden spot. In 1828,
when Jackson became president, Indian removal was imminent. Most
southern Indian groups in turn succumbed to pressure and signed removal
treaties, yielding their homelands, willingly or not, for the promise of a
new location in present-day Oklahoma.

In Wiregrass Country the removal did not proceed strictly according to
plan. Southerners were concerned not only with the acquisition of American Indian lands but also—and even more—with the perceived threat presented by African refugees on their border. The settlers voiced ongoing
concern about the loss of "property," and the Seminole Wars were the final
showdown. These wars constituted one of the longest-waged military con-

flicts in American history before the Vietnam War. Embattled bands of Seminoles and their African allies defeated all branches of the American military service in 1818 and from 1836 to 1842. The first Seminole War effected the annihilation of fringe Creek and Seminole groups in villages in outer sections of the Wiregrass. The Americans commonly used subterfuge and violated truces, using the protective white flag to capture Seminole leaders like Osceola. Africans, who faced reenslavement if they surrendered, fought as rank and file and as generals. The U.S. commander General Thomas Jesup later called the Seminole Wars "a Negro not an Indian war; and if it be not speedily put down, the South will feel the effects of it on their slave population before the end of the next season."

The stakes were considerable. Southern whites struggled to recapture the African maroons. The formerly enslaved Africans used their power with the Seminoles to defend against emigration to Oklahoma. Slaveowners demanded that government agents require Seminoles to return fugitive Africans before removal. Decisive legal action stripped the Creeks of all their lands outside Florida. Not until the Seminoles had been pacified was it said that the death knell had sounded for autonomous Creek culture. The conflict finally concluded when the U.S. Army proclaimed its end.

The Trail of Tears was one of the most heinous genocidal acts in American history. Andrew Jackson's ascendency to the presidency ended any hope of averting it. Even the acculturated Indians—those who had been unwavering in their loyalty to the white settlers—faced mass removal to Oklahoma from Wiregrass Country. Their pleas were ignored. The settlers did not want American Indians nearby on any terms. The whites' objective had always been to acquire land. Without adequate food or clothing, suffering in many cases from disease, thousands of southern Indians died while making the long trek west.

It has been estimated that only 744 Creeks remained east of the Mississippi River by the end of the nineteenth century. The U.S. government relegated the remaining Seminoles to reservations within the state of Florida. Most had died either during the Second Seminole War or en route to Oklahoma. Seminoles roamed over North Florida, hungry and desperate, and returned to their reservation only when threatened with force or enticed by the arrival of government supplies. Indians caught off the reservation were whipped and tortured. As late as the twentieth century, American Indians found in the region could be deported to Oklahoma. Indians who defied the decrees found themselves in special circumstances but remained in essence unconquered.

The place names bestowed by American Indians stand as eloquent evidence of their title to the land. Wiregrass Country owes much of its economic development to the Ocmulgee, Chattahoochee, Willacoochee, Choctawatchee, and Ochlockonee Rivers. The names alone survive as witnesses to the presence of southeastern Indians in the region.

The earliest white settlers of Wiregrass Country were chiefly emigrants from the Carolinas. As the soil became exhausted or better land was discovered, these settlers moved west. Some 94 percent of them came from English stock in the old, long-settled low country coastal plain of Georgia, South Carolina, and North Carolina. They migrated in a chainlike pattern, some taking a more circuitous route, with pioneers who relocated at a greater distance eventually resettling in Wiregrass Country near family and friends. The communities in which they settled often became known by the settlers' state of origin. Calvary, Georgia, for example, was the "North Carolina settlement." Settlers from Sampson County, North Carolina, claimed to have been told that the soil in Calvary was similar, and they expected to be able to produce the same crops. As a rule, immigrants came from similar soils and climates.

The new communities first developed rural neighborhoods, not towns. By placing their names on the landscape, they took an important step toward claiming possession. Their settlements were small but numerous: the Swamp Creek community, the Cane Water Pond community, the Hilltop community, Barnett's Creek community, and many others. Communities with claim or military offices were called districts: the Blowing Cave Militia District, the Spence District, and the Tired Creek District. Places took their names from the topography, from local churches, and from pioneer families. Because roads were poor and transportation scarce, communities formed wherever there was a store, a mill, a church, or a school.

The communities eventually imparted continuity to modern lives. Once built, houses became homes. The homes and the people who lived in them gave rise to a community personality. The homeplace, then, represents a valued family possession, an obligatory space that needs to be continuously occupied. As one descendant wrote: "The community is a better place in which to live because of them. Lotchie, who is 85, still lives at the old home place."

Settlers from Wiregrass Georgia went on to inhabit Wiregrass Alabama and Florida. The Carswell family history probably typifies the process of migration into the region. According to E. W. Carswell,

[The family] came first to Georgia and settled near Augusta about twenty-five miles south of the Hopeful Baptist Church community. They got a grant of some land from the King of England and settled there and started to try to make a living. They did very well there, I suppose. The Revolutionary War started about three years after they got there. And the old man, my great-great-great-grandfather, went to the War and one of the boys went with him.

And another of the boys disappeared at about that time from the records. I don't know what happened to him. But I think I do. He probably got killed, and it was never reported. That's a guess.

But after the War, the new government gave them some land then because of their services in the War. And some of them prospered. My own grandfather lived in Richmond County, that's the county that Augusta's in. Hopeful Church in Burke County today is where they last lived there. Then, they moved down to central Georgia, just south of Macon, Crawfords County. There was some settling in that community with some Irish people, a family named Preston. My grandpa liked to go and work for Mr. Preston on account of Mr. Preston had a daughter named Jane. So the Prestons moved to Alabama and I asked my daddy one time: "Why in the world did you all come to this little place in Alabama? (All sorts of good land around there.) Why did you come? Why didn't you go into Texas like some of the rest of them did? Why did you want to stop in Alabama?" He said, "Well, I think it was for the love of that Preston girl." So, that was the factor, I think, and they moved up to Dale County, Alabama.

They are from the heart of the Wiregrass. So, they settled up there. All their children were born there. They lived there for thirty more years and came on down to this part just inside Florida. Grandma Jane did not want to come to Florida. She told everybody that she did not want to come to this God foresaken county. It was the most dismal place. There was not many people that lived in the whole area. Finally, she told them that she agree to come, but she wanted them to promise her that when she died that they would take her back to Alabama and bury her. They did; but it wasn't saying much for Florida, was it?

Although it continued in the main to be sparsely populated, Wiregrass Country was slowly but surely transformed.

Florida continued to offer enslaved Africans a haven. While some runaways took the legendary Underground Railroad north, a body of historical legends suggests that many fugitives found refuge in the caves, swamps, and woods of their surroundings. One narrative tells how an unruly fugitive named Uncle Ben gained respect after a period of voluntary separation from his master. The coda reads: "But the strange thing was that the Marsa didn't want Uncle Ben to go back plowing. He put Uncle Ben to helping 'round the stable, and Uncle Ben didn't have to work hard no more because he had worked so hard for many years." Such tales imply by their tone that the runaways were held in greater esteem as a result of their acts of rebellion.

Wiregrass landowners proudly identified themselves as farmers rather than planters. In areas with aristocratic pretensions, a person could be considered a planter with as few as 500 acres and ten slaves. Many yeoman farmers in Wiregrass Country met this criterion and readily bought slaves as soon as they could. Economic factors, not ideology, discouraged them from generally acquiring human chattel. Indian Removal and economic underdevelopment therefore made Wiregrass Country before the Civil War essentially a white man's land.

CHAPTER 3

Agriculture, Industry, and Labor

From the last decade of the eighteenth century until the end of the Civil War, society slowly matured in the economic backwater of the Wiregrass region. The practices of the frontier in the pine belt became the rituals of settled life. Out of the remote wilderness the settlers cleared small subsistence farms for their families. Herds of cattle and hogs and flocks of sheep ranged freely to forage for themselves. People made the goods they needed and exchanged their handiwork for things they could not make. An annual or semiannual trading expedition to river or coastal ports secured necessary items that were otherwise unavailable. Over the years, a few country merchants established themselves at county seats and at way stations on the few roads that crossed the region. In addition, water mills were built at widely scattered points. These developments did not, however, greatly alter the self-sufficient character of life. The economic development of the Wiregrass region responded by degrees to the tremendous economic forces affecting the surrounding areas.

During the colonial and early national periods, subsistence agriculture dominated the entire Southeast except for a narrow strip along the Atlantic and Gulf coasts. A plantation system built on the production of indigo and naval stores and later of rice and sea island cotton developed and prospered in the coastal areas. The decline of the colonial tobacco plantations of tidewater Virginia and Maryland after the Revolution sent their proprietors in search of new lands and a new staple crop. After brief experimentation with grains and livestock, the displaced planters were drawn to cotton, a crop for which there was a great demand from the burgeoning textile industry in England.

The commercial production of cotton first centered on the coastal and river plantations of South Carolina and Georgia. The cultivation of sea island cotton on a large scale was possible only in a very limited, principally coastal area. The "green seed," or upland, cotton, although it could adapt to a much wider range of soils and climates, then required too much labor in separating the seed from the lint to be profitably produced in volume. After Eli Whitney perfected the cotton gin in 1793, the chief barrier to the resurgence of plantation agriculture was removed, and upland cotton became the major export of the southern states.

The cotton boom dictated the course of settlement and economic development in Georgia after 1793. Land speculators, planters, and farmers immediately poured into the South Atlantic states seeking the rich, heavy soils that promised an abundance of upland cotton. When the product was delivered to market, profits were enormous. The English demand was insatiable. Land hungry and labor intensive, the cotton industry sent land prices skyrocketing and revived the moribund institution of slavery. It drained the upper South of surplus slaves and drove pioneer farmers farther west or into lands of only marginal value for cotton cultivation. Within forty years of Whitney's patent, a broad belt of lands devoted primarily to the commercial production of the staple crop stretched along the lower piedmont of the seaboard states, through the new states of Alabama and Mississippi, and into Louisiana. Available cotton lands were quickly bought up and put into production. The ever-growing tide of migrants filled the new counties, however, and overflowed into the domains of the Cherokee and Creek Indians.

Settlers bypassed the Wiregrass region during the rush to western cotton lands because it was contained almost entirely by supposedly barren piney woods. Although virtually all of the region had been surveyed and organized into counties by 1820, the spreading cotton economy skirted it on all sides, allowing this area to be gradually populated, principally by stockmen and subsistence farmers. Pockets of plantation-style commercial agriculture developed, of course, on the region's boundaries, along the large river system and the "suitable lands" near Tallahassee, Florida. When the central and lower sections of the Wiregrass region opened for settlement in 1819 and 1820, they attracted migrants mainly from the upper part of the region in Georgia, many of the migrant families having originated in the coastal plain of the Carolinas. The pioneering agriculturalists included cotton planters who settled along the Ocmulgee-Altamaha and the Flint-Chattachoochee-Apalachicola Rivers. Present-day Eufaula (Alabama), Marianna (Florida), and Bainbridge and Thomasville (Georgia) reflect this heritage.

The Wiregrass region did not share in the national market revolution of the first half of the nineteenth century. Having few potential cotton-producing areas within its borders, the area did not attract the foreign and domestic investment that, in the 1830s and 1840s, built railroads from Savannah to the fall line cities of the Cotton Belt. As a result, the commerce that had previously flowed over Wiregrass rivers and roads ebbed, and the embryonic market towns, both river ports and way stations, quickly declined in importance. The region could thus access the national market only through the cotton economy.

The basic agricultural pattern of the early settlements—subsistence farming and stock raising—shifted to serve minor auxiliary functions in the cotton economy. Wiregrass farmers produced cotton in small quantities because it was the common currency of credit and trade in the Cotton Belt. Depending on the nearest market and the adaptability of their lands, farmers grew either the upland or the sea island cotton (and both in some localities). The latter was preferred because of its higher market value. Even a few bales of cotton were enough to buy the commodities, including manufactured goods, that the farmers themselves could not produce. Cotton thus protected their proceeds from other, more important transactions with the merchants and planters of the Cotton Kingdom. The settlers supplied cattle, hogs, some sheep, and later wool to the Black Belt and Tallahassee, Florida, markets. They sold farm produce as well as surplus grains and livestock to planters in relatively remote cotton areas, such as the lower Flint-Chattahoochee Valley. Whatever profits they realized were usually converted into more livestock and land.

Otherwise, the Wiregrass economy was rudimentary and self-contained. Unlike the cotton planters, who struggled to make their operations as self-sufficient as possible, the Wiregrass farmers were as free from the drawbacks of the market economy as they were from its benefits. Dr. James M. Folsom, the son of a pioneering family in Irwin County, Georgia, described the economy of the antebellum Wiregrass farm: "The pork and beef-packing house and the cloth factories and taylor-shop were in the same yard; and we could snap our fingers at tariff and interstate commerce. Even suspenders were knit or woven at home. Each farm was a joint-stock reciprocity concern and as man and wife, the business was started and usually successful." As late as 1849, a railroad promoter noted the general absence of roads and the scarcity of gristmills in the region and wrote of the simple ways of its inhabitants: "They say little, despise to be encroached upon by settlement, live on their flocks, and . . . exhibit many of the habits of the savage."

Without the pervasive influence of planters and a significant population of enslaved Africans, the social order in the Wiregrass counties kept the stamp of frontier society. Land being cheap and plentiful and settlers few, social relationships hinged upon landownership, ability, industry, family ties, and religious affiliation. A landed gentry of big farmers and prominent stockmen composed an upper class hardly distinguishable from the broad yeomanry of small farmers, herdsmen, and craftsmen. Slaves, freedman, and immigrant settlers, such as the Irish laborers who were stranded in Irwin County after an abortive attempt to construct a railroad, were so few and scattered that they were swallowed up in this homogeneous society. A small but vital professional class and a rudimentary middle class of rural merchants and businessmen originated in or aspired to the upper class. Less than 5 percent of the free population was landless or lacked significant personal property. All of the classes had the same material culture and lived in a plain, Spartan fashion. Behind its facade of impoverishment, Wiregrass society was relatively stable and free of abject want.

The gentry were the patriarchs of their respective families and the patrons of churches and fraternal orders. Its members often supplied justices of the peace and usually provided captains of the local militia. They dominated the deliberations of the grand jury and the councils of county government. Although the gentry held the political power, it rarely participated in administering law and government. Instead it left the pursuit of elective office to the lawyers (most of whom were closely tied with the gentry) and members of the professional and merchant classes. Occasionally a son of the yeomanry would ascend to a position of responsibility almost as a reminder that farmers were the source of social consensus and political power. The plain spokesmen of this class generally addressed the upper classes in family councils, church and fraternal meetings, and the spring and fall assemblies of "Big Court" at the county site. More often than not, these spokesmen also represented the landless laboring class. The process of advise and consent was effective. Aside from a disturbing tendency to violence in personal disputes, Wiregrass society was as balanced and democratic as any rural society in the nation.

As it happened, the eastern and southern extremities first gained direct access to the national market. Savannah merchants, greatly dissatisfied with their roundabout connection to the new cotton-producing areas, incorporated the Savannah and Gulf Railroad and began constructing a route through the pine flats of southeast Georgia toward the confluence of the Chattahoochee and Flint Rivers in the early 1850s. Shortly afterward, the Brunswick and Albany Railroad Company began surveying a rail line from the Atlantic port across the central Wiregrass region to Albany. The Savannah and Gulf line progressed more rapidly than its rival line and was completed almost to Thomasville at the outbreak of the Civil War. The Brunswick and Albany line was barely completed to Waresboro, Ware County, when the war intervened.

Because of the new rail connections, the counties on the southwest border of the Wiregrass region became important sources of meat and grain for the Confederate war effort. The privations wrought by the war, how-

ever, delayed the development of commercial agriculture in those and adjoining counties until the postwar years and actually reinforced the practice
of subsistence farming. The potential for the rapid commercialization of
husbandry all along the boundaries of the Wiregrass region was nevertheless present by 1861 and awaited only the reestablishment of the national
market to be realized.

The Wiregrass electorate exhibited strong opposition to secession, but
Wiregrass Country sent many of its men to fight in the Civil War. The
hostilities barely touched the region, and not having extensive slavehold-
ings or significant capital investments, the region did not suffer the physical and financial devastation of the more developed areas. The lack of farm
labor, however, and levies on crops and livestock did create real hardships
for many of the region's families. As previously noted, there was a high
rate of desertion among Wiregrass volunteers late in the conflict. The total
loss, according to the best estimate from the muster rolls, was huge as a
proportion of the sparse population. In some localities only one in every
three enlisted men returned home. Moreover, a series of local epidemics
decimated the elderly and children under ten during the late 1860s and
lengthened the lists of "blind, dumb, and idiot children." The written record of Wiregrass life, although never full, was especially scarce during the
chaotic years that followed the war. As a result, many questions concerning
the conflict's impact on the Wiregrass people remain unanswered.

When the war had finally ended, farmers in the former Confederate
states struggled to put their lands back into production. The chief difficulty
lay in securing the capital and labor necessary to make a crop. The collapse
of government and finance under the Confederacy swallowed up assets that
had been converted into bonds and currency. Subsequent laws nullified
bank charters, insurance policies, corporate stocks and bonds, and promis-
sory notes issued, endorsed, or contracted during the rebellion. The gentry
lost hundreds of millions of dollars in personal property when the enslaved
Africans were emancipated with no compensation of their former owners.
Stripped of their workforce, the planters desperately needed laborers but
lacked the resources to hire, or even to equip, their former slaves. Yeoman
farmers and other smallholders were fortunate in being able to maintain a
low level of subsistence farming. Most landless white farmers and freedmen
were destitute and unable to pay cash rent for farmland. Large-scale northern investment, although eagerly sought, did not immediately materialize.
Since the revival of transportation and commerce was slow, federal currency was scarce in the South and therefore did little to relieve the credit
problem.

After the Civil War, the farmers of the Wiregrass region found themselves gradually drawn into a national market in which domestic agricul-

ture was rapidly becoming secondary to industry and manufacturing. As they abandoned subsistence farming, they became immersed not in the revolution of the prosperous antebellum market but in the depression of the postwar economy. The growing complexities of commercial agriculture—in finance, production, transportation, marketing, and national banking and monetary policy—engulfed them and aroused their concern. In this respect the Wiregrass farmers shared the dilemma of farmers everywhere in the nation. As they became less and less able to retreat into a subsistence economy, their response to the hard times more and more followed sectional and national models.

The only commercial crop that could serve as common currency for a sharecropping system was cotton, a commodity that was in short supply because of the war. Encouraged by huge demand and familiarity with its culture and marketing, southern farmers—owners and tenants alike—planted as much of the staple as they could afford to. Their first crops were generally successful, and the usual course was to expand production under the credit system. World demand for cotton declined after 1868, however, and producers were obliged to plant more and more acreage to compensate for falling prices and rising debt. Cotton thus enslaved the southern agriculturalists. Many yeoman farmers eventually lost title to their lands and became tenants. African American smallholders, already few, found their number further reduced. The crop-lien/share tenancy system thus established a large, landless peasant class that was tied to and expanded with cotton culture.

Agricultural diversification became the catchphrase of the New South movement, but the credit system forestalled economic development and such diversification. Despite large increases in population, number of farms, and total acreage (as well as in the proliferation of market towns and industrial centers), southern agriculture regressed between 1870 and 1900, in the wake of a trend that was paradoxically tied to its expansion. Trapped in their colonial status, the southern states were but sources of raw materials for northern industries and captive markets for manufactured goods. Proponents of the New South such as Henry W. Grady saw industrial development as the means of breaking this bondage, but they showed little regard for the plight of southern agriculture and merely advised farmers to be more self-sufficient and to diversify without solving the basic problem of crop finance. As southern farmers soon realized, the New Departure would be accomplished at the expense of agriculture, which suffered economically while regional interests sought to attract commerce and industry.

The Wiregrass section in each of the three states embraced thousands of acres of cheap and unpopulated land. Many still perceived the Wiregrass

Country as valuable only for range and timber and compared it with the flat pine land of the extreme southeastern counties. As comprehensive geological surveys later showed, the forested uplands of the region harbored very promising soils that, with proper fertilization, could be as productive as the average soils of the adjoining area. Perhaps the pivotal factor, among the many forces that contributed to the agricultural development of the Wiregrass region, was the general acceptance of fertilizers in cotton culture. Promoters, seeking settlers and capital investment for the state after the war, naturally emphasized the area's advantages for the raising of stock (the production of wool), with predictable success.

Nonetheless, the expansion of the lumber and naval stores industries into the pine forests initiated the postwar development of the region. These industries stimulated railroad construction and eventually made vast tracts of cleared land available to farmers. In time, the forest industry camps and railroad installations on the main lines became market towns. Entrepreneurs, railroad companies, development concerns, and private landowners attempted to attract settlers to the new farmlands and business, professions, and trades to the towns. The less dramatic establishment of railroads and forest industries in the lower Wiregrass region at this time laid the foundation for the great rail line and town-building boom of 1885 through 1905 in all three states. Actual settlement and the establishment of the new agricultural order capped development in all areas during the years leading to World War I.

Diversification occurred in the population and industry of the Wiregrass region as well as in its agriculture. Shifts in population brought an infusion of new attitudes and material resources as well as human beings. From the Indian Removal until after Reconstruction, the region stagnated. Until the early 1880s the region's forests, sandy soils, lowlands, and lime sinks discouraged extensive settlement. Eventually, however, the region saw agricultural development with the capitalist initiative to dethrone King Cotton and diversify.

When African Americans in other parts of the South moved to large southern cities or went north, outmigration in the Wiregrass was overshadowed by immigration. The Wiregrass region offered African Americans some of the best prospects for eventual landownership. Agnes Windsor, a local African American historian, described her own family's history in Slocomb, Alabama:

Alex Johnson was born in 1835. He was from Alexandria, Virginia. Jane was born in early 1840s. She was from Tanya, Georgia. In tracking records down from Virginia and from Georgia, the meeting place had to be in Brundidge, Alabama in Pike County. Now, they got married there. But at that time Pike

County consisted of Geneva County, Dale County, and Barbour County. You see, they were split off later. So they were from Pike county up there. They were working on sharecropping. The census records show that they were sharecropping. In 1882, Alex came here with Jane and Shade Allen and some others discovering land. They had heard that there was land down here. So, they came here to see if they could homestead land. I don't know how many trips they made here to see how much of this land could they homestead. Anyway, the families moved here in 1882 and established this place. Now, they already had children who were grown and married. Because my grandmother, who was Sally, was already married. She had married Joe Miller before coming here. And there were some others in the family also married. It was about fourteen of my father's people. You had to stay here five years before you could homestead your land. So, my grandfather made his homestead papers. He had to name everything that he had. He was worth $130 in 1882.

During the antebellum period in the Wiregrass, whites outnumbered blacks three to one. By 1880, in many parts, the African American presence had shifted the ratio to two to one. Tenacity paid off for the richest in terms of land ownership.

According to some observers, economic enrichment has always been the main incentive for population shifts within the United States. The boll weevil drove many weary Black Belt residents into Wiregrass Country. Family histories published in Grady County, Georgia, show that some white residents attribute their presence to a trend in 1917. "A group was sent to Grady County and wrote back such good reports that we were part of a mass migration of about fifty families, including two doctors. They moved by wagon train into the area. For these families, this was called, 'the Great Migration.'" One former resident of Henry County, Alabama, said he heard that the land in Grady County was "rich and fertile." He came, he liked what he saw, and he bought a farm.

The stereotype of the Wiregrass farmer faded as the term "diversified farmer" came into vogue. The new coinage denoted not just an idea but a commitment to an agricultural way of life. The small farm represented the region's backbone. Although money had continuously been in short supply, little had been needed until the past few decades. Residents participated in a local barter system that reduced the demand for legal tender. "People went to town only occasionally and carried a few chickens and eggs, a piece or two of meat, or maybe a barrel of syrup and bought the necessaries of life." The indispensable items usually included staples such as flour, sugar, coffee, and rice that could not be grown at home. Life histories suggest that there was essentially no hunger. Pearly Broome, a lifelong resident of Grady County, commented, "We put up everything that we put our hands on." People also left goods in payment for services rendered, for example, by the millers. Ann Malone says that the farmers were "more free of genuine poverty than most."

The herding of cattle was one of the oldest folklife practices in Wiregrass Country. The herders' dependence on the open range method of cattle raising dated to their immigration (mainly from Carolina) and illustrated the intricate interaction of culture and environment. "Cracker cowboys," or "cowmen," as they were called, raised scrub cattle primarily for the Cuban and European markets. Like the ritual burning of forests, the cattle-herding tradition died hard. Olin Pope, a third-generation white farmer in Barwick, Georgia, recalled the annual cow hunts across the open range near his home:

> They had [an African American] Jim Ryan out there. He had a lot of cows. Well, my grandfather and father had a lot of cows. And . . . when Jim would get ready to round up his cows, he'd come over and tell grandpa. He'd say, "We are going to have a round up day." He'd get some of grandpa's cows and granpa'd get some of his cows, but they got them all in a pen. Then, the round up is when they sold cows. What grandpa had at this place, belonged to Jim, he'd load them up first and then go over to Jim's place and finish getting what he was going to sell, his mark in the ear. And they would do grandpa the same way. They knew how many cows they sold. What calves they had then they just divided them. There was no troubles.

By 1953, however, free-ranging animals were illegal in all of Wiregrass Country.

In the 1890s tobacco began to be regarded as a chief crop in part of the Wiregrass. This crop created a great southern industry that eventually supplied the entire country. The prospect of growing tobacco attracted more North Carolinians to the region, and eventually their gamble paid off. Farmers promoted two types, flue tobacco and shade tobacco. The latter was unique to Wiregrass Georgia and Florida. It grew in an area roughly twenty-five miles long and twenty miles wide. The tobacco was grown under cheesecloth and produced leaves used exclusively for the outside wrapper of cigars. Early developers called it brown gold.

The cheesecloth covering shade tobacco served several purposes. According to Carolyn Chason, now a local historian in Grady County and the daughter of the supervisor on a shade tobacco farm, "It filtered the sun. The tobacco leaves were thin. It also protected them from insects because, I'm sure you've been told, . . . you wanted flawless tobacco leaves since it was for the outside wrapper. And everybody had to be very careful and watch for your worms. Another thing the shades would do was protect the crops from hail in the summer time because a hail storm would ruin the

A shade tobacco worker
hoes young plants grown
under cheesecloth, c. 1966.
Photo by Paul Kwilecki.
Reproduced by permission.

crop. It was a fast growing crop." Young adults vied for jobs harvesting the crop. Since the work was done by groups, young people considered it a diversion. When cigar manufacturing declined, farmers stopped growing shade tobacco.

Today the peanut remains the region's preeminent crop. From the outset it did not require much labor and sold at adequate prices. Farmers relied on it originally to fatten their hogs. In time the peanut came to be used in a variety of consumer products and grew in popularity. By the 1930s peanuts had come to be regarded as a key crop that qualified farmers for government benefits. Several Wiregrass towns now vie for the title "Peanut Capital of the World."

Wiregrass landowners developed various ways of acquiring revenue to maintain their farms. Some grew timber. Others distilled their own turpentine for market and acted as their own chipper, scraper, and dipper. One man, according to one of folklorist Mariella Hartsfield's informants, "worked for about a fifteen-year interval managing A&P grocery stores [while remaining] first and last the farmer, loving the land and prizing the means of working the land—whether it was his mules in the early days or his Ford tractor in his later years."

Naval stores represented one of the earliest commercial enterprises intro-

With diversification, peanuts became a major crop in the Wiregrass economy. Photo by Jerrilyn McGregory.

duced into the area. Men heated the gum from trees to produce a pitch resin that was used to caulk the seams of wooden ships, hence the name "naval stores." Turpentine, the residue from this distilling operation, did not become valuable until later. Migrants came to Wiregrass Country to operate turpentine stills and worked as woods hands, woods riders, coopers, and tallymen. The names given the various workers amounted to job descriptions: stillers, deckhands, haulers, dippers, and chippers. Dippers emptied the cups of gum into buckets. Tallymen kept count of the number of "streaks," or the amount of gum, that each worker dipped. The count determined each man's pay. The haulers' job was to bring the gum turpentine to the distillery in a wagon that had tall wheels to help it straddle stumps. The cooper built and repaired barrels for the spirits and rosin. The stiller worked at the hand-fired still. This usually consisted of a large copper cauldron encased in a masonry furnace crowned with a bulbous cap that was connected to a spiraling, wormlike pipe inside the cooling tank. E. W. Carswell recalled, "By listening to the end of the worm pipe, a good stiller could tell by the bubbling sound coming from the cooking turpentine in the cauldron if it was cooking too fast, too slow or just right." African Americans performed most of the tasks of the wood hands. The woods rider—the white superintendent—rode on horseback through the woods

A turpentine mill. Photo courtesy of Vanishing Georgia, Georgia Department of Archives and History, Atlanta.

to inspect their work. Woods riders rode one horse in the morning and a fresh one in the afternoon.

White residents often nostalgically recall the songs that, as children, they heard sung by the African American turpentine workers. Writer Clifton Johnson said, "Often you hear them . . . in the distance singing some old racial folk-song that has neither beginning nor end, but which, in its strange cadences, chimes in with the music of the wind in the treetops." Carswell, too, spoke of sounds he remembered when he returned home after World War II. The smell of turpentine, which somewhat resembled that of limburger cheese, conjured up memories of the "melodic calls and responses of black men as they had worked during the humid summer months among the tall pines. The language was their own." Owen Wrice, an African American, worked as a turpentiner when he was a young man and described the chants:

> Every individual out there whenever they were hoeing them boxes they had a call sign. Like "L.E." or "15" or "75," "Johnny" or "Jerry," whatever your number . . . word was. When you hollered that out, the man would mark you down a tree then. See you had finished up a tree. And then you would go to another tree, and you'd begin to hoe out that tree. And when you get that tree completed, then you holler 75 or 15 whatever your number was. And he'd tally

you up; and see at the end of the day, you'd go up to him. And he would tell you how many trees you were at, and they would pay you so much per tree.

The calls were rhythmically rendered and sung by lone workers to break the monotony.

For landless people, whatever their race, wage labor afforded another weapon against the cycle of poverty. Workers in the forest industry lived on the rails. Twenty men at a time slept in double-decker bunks called "Shaking Jacobs." Able to visit their families only on Sundays, the men ate family style from a lunch and dinner menu consisting of beans, boiled meat, and cornbread. Although the races were segregated, everyone earned the same meager wages. Workers labored at their own risk, and since there was no concern for employee safety, catastrophes were frequent. Trains often derailed on the poorly maintained lines, and the boilers of sawmills routinely exploded.

Some workers were able to supplement their wages by working for the numerous nurseries that sprang up with the growth of the pecan industry. Like the peanut, the pecan helped stabilize the agricultural economy of the region. Cultivation and harvest were a family affair, but operators had first to set aside land for the pecan orchards and then to wait years while the trees reached maturity. For those who persevered, the gamble paid off. Today pecan merchants are numerous and the industry healthy. Even those who own but a few trees in their yards are able to market their crop. The nurseries diversified by growing other ornamental plants.

The shift of farmers to new occupations was most evident in light manufacturing within the region. Processing plants brought the closest thing to industrial jobs. Textile mills and other heavy manufacturers did not operate in the Wiregrass. The life experiences of Albert Daniel Brinson, one resident, are perhaps representative of the era after World War II. "I worked at various trades: farming, sawmilling, carpentry, and pecan planting. I worked in a casket factory, barrell [*sic*] factory, and in the Campbell soup factory." Local residents benefited most from internal processing and distribution plants, which refined produce near home before shipping it out. Many residents were able to retire with their farms intact. Some children who were born after 1950 reached adulthood in the Wiregrass without ever seeing a cotton boll.

Despite the hardships, most landowners struggled to maintain their autonomy and continued to practice a lifestyle characterized by interdependent caring and sharing. One Wiregrass native remarked: "People say, 'come and pick peanuts out of my field, I'm fixing to plow it under, come and pick peanuts and boil them'; or they'll say, 'You have a standing invitation to fish from my pond. I'll tell you where the best fishing places are.'

We have people like that, you just love them to death. You go to your front door and there's some vegetables somebody just brought in. Sometimes they don't even let you know they were here." Altruism was second nature, and no one thought twice about offering to help a sick friend. Tommie Gabriel, a lifelong resident of Thomas County, Georgia, explained that, in the African American community, "if a man, for example on a farm, got his leg broke or something happened, he got sick. Those people come over there and dig his farm, give him a day's work. They would all cook dinner and have dinner together and move on. His crops went right along with the other's crop. Now that's the way they survived so that no one had to suffer." Wiregrass Country was far from being an impersonal space.

The agricultural regions of the South, in general, never attracted foreign immigrants in large numbers. As in Wiregrass Country, for the most part the original settlers poured in from adjoining states rather than from foreign shores. There are several possible reasons: inferior economic opportunities, an uncongenial social climate, and xenophobia. Before the Civil War, Wiregrass Country appealed principally to those who had money with which to buy land. Few opportunities existed for employment. The situation was far from stagnant, however.

Life changed significantly with the arrival of the industrialists, and the railroad served as catalyst. Migrants and immigrants alike began coming in large numbers. Before the appearance of railroad lines, considerations of social class drew little attention in the Wiregrass. A business or professional class was slow to develop until the advent of trains. Towns themselves did not really exist until about 1890, when the railroads constructed tracks and stations. Economic change in general, and industrialism in particular, highlighted racial and class tensions and the disparity in legal rights between the African Americans and the white settlers. Many of the laws that adversely affected African Americans discouraged immigrants, many of whom sought equality as well as freedom.

Despite the obstacles, Jewish immigrants launched a largely successful campaign in several Wiregrass towns. In about 1904 one merchant placed the following ad in the *Cairo Messenger*: "A NEW JEW STORE! I beg to announce to the people of Cairo, Ga., that I have opened up a General Merchandise Store, consisting of Dry Goods, Notions and Fancy Groceries, and will sell everything as cheap as any body and respectfully solicit the patronage of every one. Those who patronize me will find themselves treated nicely in every respect. Come and give me a call." A century ago, Cairo's largest neighbor, Thomasville, had about forty-two Jewish merchants. Beginning in about 1885, they immigrated mainly from Germany and Eastern Europe, at a time when many Wiregrass towns were just being founded. The wares offered by these merchants improved the quality of life for everyone. Socially they met with acceptance in some spheres and discrimination in others.

Although Jewish American communities soon formed congregations and built synagogues, the people were generally unable to observe their faith fully. A rabbi could visit only once a month. The faithful found that they needed to travel to observe certain holidays or to have other ritual acts performed. The observance of important rituals and traditions required leadership and action. Over time, congregations dwindled, because many Jewish American children, following a general trend, chose to leave the Wiregrass region.

In recent years, however, the population of new immigrants has risen. The region now relies on Latino migrant farm laborers to harvest several key crops. Many of them are choosing to settle in the area permanently. Their presence brings new business and creates new markets in small rural towns. The Latino presence is apparent in supermarket offerings, in the stock of local department stores, and even in the raising of goats by local farmers. Some members of the Latino population are opening restaurants and bakeries to cater to their ethnic community.

As these migrants make contact with the broader community, several stereotypes come under attack. Although the laborers are regarded as Mexican, in reality some of them come from El Salvador, Guatemala, Cuba, other Central American countries, and Haiti. (The Haitians have not yet begun to settle in large numbers.) Rather than being exclusively Catholic, as they are presumed to be, many are Protestants, having been converted by missionaries in their homelands. Some of the newcomers seek to join Methodist, Pentecostal, Church of Christ, and Jehovah's Witness congregations. They may need separate religious services because of language barriers or because they work on Sunday mornings. Some churches, as part of their outreach, offer bilingual services at special times.

The Latino population is already a significant force in several Wiregrass communities, which have grown to depend on the immigrants' labor and business. Their presence has not been without problems, however. Housing costs routinely skyrocket during the weeks when migrant labor crews live in an area. Some communities have greeted them with hostility, discrimination, and some persecution. In the main, however, the new immigrants encounter a quiet acceptance much like that which greeted the Jews and the Catholics. The Latinos represent a small, productive minority, and the region on the whole appears to be adapting to the new multiculturalism.

Other new groups have also begun to arrive. East Indians are now operating many motels, often with banquet facilities, and Chinese entrepreneurs have opened several restaurants. Near Panama City and Dothan, Alabama, and near Valdosta, Georgia, these groups rival the Latinos in size. With its cultural stress on self-sufficiency and self-containment, the Asian American community tends to be less visible than the Latino but is equally diverse. The East Indians are often South African expatriates who have few ties to India and more than a passing familiarity with African peoples. By the same token, the Asian Americans include not only Chinese Americans but also Koreans and Japanese and are American born.

As many as 74,000 American Indians are also present and live chiefly in loose associations in the South today. The Poarch Creeks, who live one county away from the historic Wiregrass, are perhaps representative. At the time of removal, they included many members of mixed blood and were deemed "friendly Creeks." A few bands were permitted to stay and were granted land. In violation of ancient custom, many of them intramarried, probably in response to their isolation and the perceived threat from outside. The white community in Wiregrass Florida called the offspring of American Indian and African parents "domineckers," after a breed of rooster with some brown feathers and some black. The Jim Crow laws of the post-Reconstruction South were applied to these Indian people and were used to defraud them of land. They customarily chose to attend their own segregated schools.

A growing number of distant descendants of the original Creek Nation are today claiming an American Indian identity. In so doing they meet with resistance from individuals and groups continuously recognized as American Indians. Indian people who were once removed to Oklahoma and who have been authenticated by the Bureau of Indian Affairs claim a historical identity as well as a genetic one. The other faction, however, has achieved state recognition more readily but will probably never be recognized nationally. This group has few physical traits that would distinguish its members from Europeans and is quite diverse in genetic makeup. Its members are accused sometimes of romanticizing their Indian connection in today's relatively receptive cultural climate and sometimes of seeking to exploit affirmative action funding programs designed to benefit minorities.

Many newly self-proclaimed American Indians, lacking genetic proof of their ancestry, gain federal recognition on the basis of family folklore. This family folklore commonly states that they concealed their Indian heritage so that they could remain in the Wiregrass or that they returned from Oklahoma or Texas at later dates. Concealment was of course possible because of their acculturation and mixed racial heritage. According to Andrew Ramsey's acknowledgment application, "Despite the official removal policy, Creeks scattered throughout the West Florida panhandle." His petition indicates that racial mixing was often a deliberate decision. Sarah Smith, whose father was considered mestizo, urged her son, "Get out, get a job, learn, and if you can, marry into the whites."

One group has reconstructed a reservation in Whigham, Georgia, that it calls Tama, after the postconquest name given to the Ocmulgee Big Bend region. De Soto probably entered the original location, thought to be Pine Island in western Dougherty County, Georgia. Some 150 years later, the Tama people apparently moved to the Apalachee region of Florida and became one of the nations forming the Seminoles. Critics argue that the present-day group is fraudulent, because its claims conflict with history. Those who have benefited feel, however, that the group, having secured state recognition, affords some cultural unity for descendants who cannot travel far to participate in ceremonies and rituals. Other groups in Wiregrass Country have also achieved their state's certification. The Florida Tribe of Eastern Creek Indians administers to ten counties of the Florida panhandle east of Pensacola. The Alabama Indian Affairs Commission has recognized several groups in Wiregrass Alabama: the Machis Lower Creek, the Cherokees of southeast Alabama, and the Star Clan of Muscogee Creeks.

Finally, the original Creek Nation in Oklahoma wishes to return home, east of the Mississippi River, for spiritual reasons. An annual powwow at Chehaw State Park may be paving the way for a land grant in Georgia. In addition, a debate rages over ownership of a casino in the Florida panhandle. The prospect that removed Indians will return arouses animosity among descendants who lack national recognition and who cannot participate in certain Creek events that may require a Bureau of Indian Affairs identification card. The century and a half of experience that divides the two groups cannot easily be bridged. One side argues, "You could have stayed if you tried"; the other retorts, "You did not endure the hardship and the pain." For each group, the Green Corn ceremony captures the essence of Indianness. Those who lack access to "authentic" ceremonies create their own and continue to hope that the two factions will find common ground and transcend their past.

Despite the influx of the new groups and former residents, Wiregrass Country remains sparsely populated and economically depressed by national standards. Many of its counties fall near the bottom of every statistical indicator. The region has been able to diversify, however, in relation to its natural environment, its crops, and its people. This achievement is emblematic both of flexibility needed for future development and of the original diversity and interdependence of the Wiregrass region. Long before the arrival of de Soto and his men, the longleaf pine, the red cockaded woodpecker, and wiregrass, in combination, sustained the ecosystem while protecting the attributes and survival needs of each constituent member.

PART TWO

Words, Music, and the Oral Tradition

CHAPTER 4

Rafthands of the Altamaha River

The river called Altamaha winds through 140 miles of south Georgia's wiregrass and piney woods. It is surely one of America's most overlooked natural resources, neglected by historians, folklorists, and even naturalists. And it is a lot of river. Draining a watershed of 14,530 square miles, the Altamaha accounts for the largest outflow of water in the Southeast. On the Atlantic coast, only the Chesapeake Bay empties more fresh water into the ocean.

One reason for the Altamaha's relative obscurity may be its rural location. The river begins, meanders, and ends hundreds of miles from Georgia's population center. Residents of north and central Georgia know and love the Chattahoochee or Savannah or Oconee Rivers. These three lesser streams, however, have all been dammed, misdirected, and overused to provide day trippers with opportunities for water games and commercial amusements. The Altamaha, on the other hand, offers conventional thrill seekers no prepackaged entertainment. Developers of recreational facilities find it unprofitable to capitalize on an undammed river, especially one that lacks whitewater.

The largest river in the Southeast begins in a remote corner of the south Georgia Wiregrass, where Montgomery, Jeff Davis, and Wheeler Counties meet. The spot cannot be reached by public roads, and people seldom go there. The best way to see it is by canoe. Whether you approach by way of the Oconee or the Ocmulgee River, you see the same thing: two major tributaries collide head-on in a broad vortex of seething water.

The sight has caused observers to marvel. A solitary canoeist might linger for hours. At "the Forks," however, as the locals know it, one is never truly alone. Two hundred feet overhead, the swallowtail kite circles. The turkey strolls along the sandbar and tolerates quiet visitors, unlike the pileated woodpecker, whose deep, sharp warning echoes across the turbulent waters.

The Oconee and the Ocmulgee start tentatively in north Georgia. At first quiet springs, they become fledgling creeks and steadily broaden, gathering speed, as they course through the state's northeastern and central hills. In contrast, the Altamaha instantly rises as a full-grown giant from a dark whirlpool in a remote forest northeast of Hazlehurst and south of Uvalda.

From the Forks to the coast, a serpentine expanse leads into hundreds of miles of dark and quiet swamps, which become six miles wide in fall and winter, when rains cause the river to overflow its banks. During spring and summer, the waters recede and lay bare hundreds of sandbars flanked with willows. Also revealed are new channels across the landscape. Each winter's powerful waters eliminate sharp bends in the river, thereby creating oxbow lakes that eventually fill with sediment and with cypress, sweet gum, and willow trees. The river affords an ever-expanding nursery for rare plants and animals. To the casual observer, the abundance of natural resources in this part of the Wiregrass is stupefying.

Part of the river's historical identity, however, is not evident to the casual observer today. It once served as a cradle for the first Americans and the first towns. Elderly women and men in the late twentieth century have stories to tell and songs to sing of the Altamaha. By listening carefully, we can learn of traditions that reflect family life and local culture and, on a broader scale, the history of the timber industry.

The customs of the timber trade bind together the entire Altamaha river valley. At its center stand rafthands, frontiersmen who once built and navigated timber rafts from Lumber City down the Altamaha to the international timber port of Darien on the Atlantic coast. The enterprise itself has vanished, but its traces linger in the collective memory of the people.

As recently as the 1970s and 1980s, octogenarians from the Altamaha river valley spoke of the days when they and their fathers ran timber. They rode rafts to Darien, which from the 1870s to the 1920s exported timber in quantity to Europe and especially to the British Isles. The work of the raftsmen was similar to that of shanty boys in the North. They had the same skills as lumberjacks and knew how to use the peavey, hook, and jam. Nevertheless, they had a culture distinct from that of the woodsmen of Maine and Michigan in almost every way. Their headquarters was the family farm, and they knew nothing of the shanty town.

Rafting took place on a number of American rivers in the nineteenth and early twentieth centuries, but the design of the Altamaha timber raft (figure 3) is unique. The sharp end allowed the raft to glance off the numerous points of land that reach into the river channel. A rectangular or square

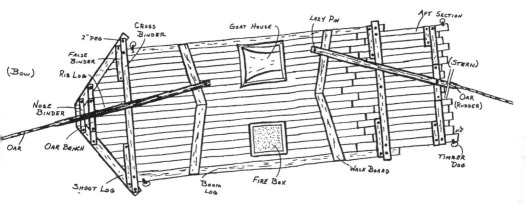

Fig. 3   Altamaha Sharp-Shooter by Hugh Darley.

raft of the sort then a familiar sight on other rivers would easily have broken up after hitting one of the Altamaha's many turning points.

According to author Brainard Cheney, the first serious efforts to build a lumber mill in Lumber City, Georgia, failed in the 1840s because the owners built rafts that followed the popular American model. Cheney credited an anonymous farmer from Telfair County with developing the "Sharp Shooter" in the early 1870s, thereby reviving the rafting industry.

The pilot of a raft often hired someone to serve as cook. Occasionally families undertook the preparation and navigation of rafts, and wives cooked food for husbands and children. Occasionally, too, pilots would cook for the rafthands. Three essential utensils were a coffee pot, a spider (an iron skillet with three legs), and a stew pot (sometimes a large, disposable tin can or a lard bucket). Novelist Kirk Munroe described the rafthands' typical fare: "fried catfish, just from the river, home smoked bacon, hominy ground in a steel mill nailed to a pine tree, where the corn is put through once for 'grits' and twice for meal, fresh cane syrup, hot pones, and black coffee."

Because the Altamaha's channel changes seasonally, farmers sending crops downriver depended upon pilots who knew the idiosyncrasies of the numerous bends. A savvy pilot would know which points of land to avoid, for example, and which to hug. In 1982, according to Bill Deen, a former pilot, the proper maneuver depended "on where the current runs." Looking back on his years on the river, from 1900 to 1930, Deen said, "You've got to know the river, really know the river. You keep the bow close to the bank if the current runs up by a point." What if the stern crashes into the riverbank after you pass the point? "You let her slam, by God, but you better keep the bow in the current," Deen replied.

Brainard Cheney, who served as a rafthand in about 1915, recalled two difficult spots on the Altamaha. "Point Pull Away" required the rafthands to pull the oars hard, forcing the raft onto the opposite side of the river where the channel was deep. "Point Pull Away and Be Damned" reminded them to hug the point as they continued downstream.

The Altamaha community esteemed experienced and successful pilots. Farmers with large holdings of timber maintained friendships with pilots such as Bill Deen, John Rewis, Ed Anderson, Will Bowen, Jesse Yeomans, and Tobe Vaughan. Likewise, timber merchants at the Darien docks often gave preferential treatment to the pilot who was honest about the quality of the timber he carried.

Home communities regarded experienced pilots highly as well. Some were active in civic affairs and held public office. Others preferred the solitude of life on the river. Bill Deen concentrated exclusively on his work during the early part of his life. Rafthands were paid in accordance with their skill and strength—in the 1920s, according to Bill Deen, the equivalent of three to five dollars a day, depending on the length of the trip and the size of the raft. These were better than average wages by regional standards at that time. During summer and fall months, when the water was too low for rafting, Deen tended crops at his farm, fished, and hunted.

Deen was regarded as a premier raft pilot, one of the best ever to run timber to the sea, and as a superior outdoorsman. In the 1930s, after rafting had ceased to be a way of life, he worked as a riverboat pilot and surveyor while maintaining the family farm at Deen's Landing, about ten miles north of Baxley on the Altamaha's south side, which had been in his family for three generations. He died in 1985 at the age of ninety-three. *Lamb in His Bosom*, a novel by Baxley native Caroline Miller that won the 1935 Pulitzer Prize, mentions timber rafting by farmers who resemble members of the Deen family.

The pilot "calls the shots, and the rafthand does the work," Deen said. "When I say 'bow white,' that means the fellow at the bow puts his shoulder to the sweep and pushes the raft to the north side. When I say 'bow Injun,' you push and pull to the south side." The terms arose during Georgia's frontier history when the Altamaha was the boundary separating the settlers from the Creek Indians. Until the 1830s, territory south of the Alta-

A riverboat on the Ocmulgee River. Photo courtesy of Vanishing Georgia, Georgia Department of Archives and History, Atlanta.

maha belonged to the Creek Nation. Like many of the river's place names, the terms used by rafthands before the Civil War originated with operators of pole boats and cotton barges who traveled from Darien to Macon or Dublin and points in between.

Kirk Munroe's popular historical novel of 1899, *Shine Terrill, A Sea Island Ranger,* was set in the lower Altamaha river valley. It describes a familiar episode in the daily life of the rafthand:

> Finally a black man loomed out of the darkness, the light resolved itself into a fire that seemed to burn on the surface of the river, the voices shouted intelligible words, and Terrill knew that one of the great timber rafts, such as float by hundreds down the Altamaha and its tributary streams to feed the devouring sawmills of the coast, was drifting by him. As it moved slowly past where he sat, delicious odors of frying bacon and boiling coffee were wafted up from the fire, where the raft cook was preparing supper. . . . All at once a voice from its extreme aft end cried out: "Bow Injun! Work her insho' Marse Ross. We'se gotter tie up somewhar long hyar kase dey's a rip jes roun' de nex' pint what needs daylight fer to run."

In the 1970s and 1980s, Delma Presley interviewed a half dozen former pilots, all of whom were white. He was unable to find any African Americans who had served as pilots. As the passage quoted above indicates, however, Munroe depicted African American pilots and rafthands. Deen remembered one. "Now John was a colored man. I tell you what. He hadn't been to school, but he was smart as he was strong. And he would stick with you. Boy-oh-boy, he was just like a brother . . . , one of the best rafthands I ever had."

African American workmen on the coast provided the muscle for loading the rafthands' timber. They were overseen by stevedores, who might be white or black. The timber loaders created songs that helped a dozen individuals coordinate their efforts as they heaved cargo into three-masted schooners in the port at Darien. In 1973, James Cook, a former stevedore and an active lay leader in the Baptist church, recalled his days as a stevedore. The men depended on the work song, he said, because it "gave them the power . . . to pull and push." Like many work songs, Cook's favorite was composed of lyrics that fit various melodies or could become a sing-song chant:

> I'm a noble soldier,
> Soldier of the jubilee.
> I'm getting old and crippled in my knee,
> Soldier of the cross.

"When they sing 'Soldier of the jubilee,' they know that it's time for every horse to pull," said Cook. "The whip is behind him if he don't pull." When they sang the last line of the song, according to Cook, "that piece of timber must move, I'm saying, when you pull it. Amen!"

In the 1970s Bessie Jones and the Sea Island Singers revived one popular song of the timber docks.

> Pay me, oh pay me, *pay me my money down.*
> Pay me or go to jail, *pay me my money down.*
> Think I hear my captain say, *pay me my money down,*
> "Tomorrow is my sailing day," *pay me my money down.*
> Pay me, oh pay me, *pay me my money down.*
> Pay me, Mr. Stevedore, *pay me my money down.*
> One of these days I going away, *pay me my money down,*
> Won't be back till Judgement Day, *pay me my money down.*
> Pay me, oh pay me, *pay me my money down.*
> Pay me or go to jail, *pay me my money down.*
> Wish I was Mr. Dodge's son, *pay me my money down,*
> Stay in the house and drink good rum, *pay me my money down.*
> Pay me, oh pay me, *pay me my money down.*
> Pay me or go to jail, *pay me my money down.*

The refrain "pay me my money down" cued the workmen to pull the timber in unison. Such work songs also represented the only form of protest African American laborers could register to ridicule those who exploited them.

The tools of the rafthand were few and relatively light: a two-inch auger for drilling holes in timbers, in case the raft needed repairs; an axe; and rope for securing the raft to the bank at nightfall. Optional but useful implements were a peavey (a "push pole" for moving timbers around) and several timber dogs. The latter, made by blacksmiths, were sharp iron spikes measuring eight to ten inches with a six-inch circle of iron attached at the blunt end. Rafthands would drive the spike into a timber that drifted beneath the surface and secure it to high-floating pieces by tying a rope to the circle of iron.

The last essential piece of equipment was the maul—a large, heavy wooden hammer made from a hard, nongrainy wood such as gum or tupelo. The handle, about two feet long and two inches in diameter, was attached to a heavy, rounded wooden piece made of a sixteen-inch section of hardwood log about twelve inches in diameter. A typical maul weighed fifteen or twenty pounds and was discarded when the raft reached its destination.

By the time they reached Darien, the rafthands were bearded and sooty from the cooking fire. They coiled their rope around one shoulder. On the other they strapped the spider and coffee pot. The axe they hung from their belts. If they had a gun or an auger, they slung it over one shoulder. Residents of Darien heard the metallic clanging of rafthands a long way off and sometimes looked upon them with condescension.

The disdain of the locals reflected cultural pride. Scottish Highlanders had established Darien in 1735, some fifty years before Scotch-Irish (former Scots Lowlanders) began moving into the Wiregrass. The long-standing enmity between the backwoods crackers and coastal aristocrats had its roots in Britain, where both Highlanders and the English had given the name "cracker" to Scots Lowlanders and Scotch-Irish. (In the Scottish language, a cracker was a boaster, jokester, and independent spirit.)

Rafthands sometimes frequented one or another of Darien's two dozen bars and pleasure houses. Eventually they began the long walk home. Some booked passage on the ferries *Daisy* and *Hessie*, which carried them as far as Brunswick. If they were really fortunate, they then boarded a train that carried them nearer their homes in the backwoods.

Rafthands and pilots formed a temporary close-knit community while they worked their way toward the sea. James Rollison served as a rafthand in the early 1900s, when he was in his teens and early twenties. His native village in Toombs County, Ohoopee, is within a stone's throw of the Ohoopee River, which empties into the Altamaha near Reidsville, Georgia.

In 1972, while describing his youth, Mr. Rollison noted that the experience with timber and rafting was his initiation into manhood.

On his maiden rafting voyage down the Ohoopee, Rollison was required to tear off his shirttail and tie it to a tree at a place called Shirt Tail Bend. On the Altamaha, experienced rafthands forced him to "treat the willows" at Rag Point, some thirty-five miles above Darien. If he failed to do so, according to rafthand tradition, he "would have bad luck and might even die before [he] reach[ed] Darien. It was a serious business, Rag Point was." Rollison continued: "I've seen the willows covered with all sorts of clothing: bandanas, shirt tails, long johns, even a pair of overalls."

Kirk Munroe's historical novel traces a character's dramatic difficulties to his failure to "treat the point":

> Late in the afternoon the pilot called out that "Rag Point" was in sight, and bade everyone on board make ready to sacrifice to the river gods some article of clothing, no matter how trifling or worthless it might be.
>
> As the raft was held close in to the "white" bank, which was here low and fringed with willows, a stretch of nearly a mile was seen to be hung with the fluttering rags of cast-off garments left there by passing raftsmen. All on board excepting Terrill had made provision for this emergency, and as the raft swept under the overhanging branches they flung their offerings into them.
>
> "Frow somefin! Frow somefin! Marsh Shine!" admonished the pilot, "less'n you'll get into a heap o' trubble befo' de day ober."
>
> But our lad had nothing save the clothing in which he stood, and sturdily chose to defy the threatened evil rather than part with any of it. All of his comrades, including Mr. Ross, urged him to follow the custom of the river; but he would not, and at length the opportunity for doing so was lost.

Another ritual for novice rafthands involved the use of the maul after the raft trip had ended. The pilot would order the initiate to carry the maul around Darien as the crew visited local stores or saloons. Within a day or two, the pilot and crew would begin the walk home—a journey of as much as 125 miles or more by road and forest trails. James Rollison recalled: "After we had walked for a day, about twenty miles, the pilot looked at me and gave out a big laugh: 'what you doing with that maul on your shoulder? Throw that thing away. We'll make another one when we build the next raft!' Then everybody burst out into laughter. . . . I tell you, I didn't think it was funny." Rafthands carried home the more valued gear, however, including the spider, the coffee pot, the auger, the rope, provisions for meals, and merchandise purchased at one of Darien's stores. Brainard Cheney recalled part of a song about rafthands:

> Rope around my shoulder
> Auger in my hand

> And a little brown jug
> From Darien.

James Rollison throughout his life remembered these lines:

> Ain't gonna live in the country.
> Ain't gonna live in the town.
> Gonna wait right here till the river rises,
> And run my timber down.

The tune was that of "Get Along Home, Cindy," he recalled, and many of that song's familiar lyrics appeared in the rafthands' version. According to Rollison, however, the most memorable music made by the rafthands was the wordless river holler.

> Well, that river holler. It is rather plaintive, especially at dark, or just before dark—you know, when you're gonna tie up. I think it has the same effect on you it did to me—as a bell or a gong or a whistle would have on a dog. You ever seen a dog sit down and howl? I don't know what it does to him, but he'll do it. And I tell you, it'll just make your hair stand on your head, if you know how to do it. . . . Late in the evening your voice seems to travel farther and clearer and more distinct than it would any other time. It wouldn't have that effect in the morning, that's for sure.

When he demonstrated the river holler in 1972, Rollison's voice filled the room with four notes of alternating joy and mournfulness that lasted altogether less than one minute. When Rollison was asked to explain why the rafthands used this distinctive combination of sounds, he said:

> Well, I don't know. It was saying good bye to the end of a hard day in your own fashion. And you made everybody else a little happier. When ol' John Rewis would start hollering that river holler, everybody would shut up. If they were whisperin', they'd shut up. And I want to tell you, it affected me. It would almost make you cry. If you weren't so hard-hearted and inured to hardships and everything else, you'd cry.

While rafthands perpetuated river place names used by the antebellum pole boaters, they also left a large number of new names and explanations for them. Place names associated with the rafthands pepper the U.S. Geological Survey map of the Altamaha. People who live in the river valley know and use many of the names that are losing currency among cartographers: Jacks Suck, Tar Landing, Kneebuckle Bend, Sister Pine Round, Old Hell Bight, Mad Dog Island, and Alligator Congress. Devil's Elbow designated several sharp turns that tested a pilot's skills. "Many a raft of timber has broken up at Devil's Elbow," according to Brainard Cheney. Each name evokes lore as revealing about those who named the places as about the places themselves.

Several former raftsmen chuckled when they were asked about Old Woman's Pocket and Devil's Shot Bag, both located in the same general area. Jesse Yeomans said, "A woman waded across the river when the water was low. Somebody asked her how deep it was, and she said it 'came up to my pocket.' Later an old devil of a fellow crossed the river, and said, 'yeah, it was deep enough to come up to my shot bag.' " The double meaning was not lost on travelers who used these place names.

Rafthands recalled stories of mishaps and tragedies on the river at places such as Deadman's Point. Only a skilled pilot could negotiate the deceptive currents of Buggs Suck and avoid submerged obstacles, such as Cotton Box. General James Oglethorpe, the founder of the colony of Georgia, allegedly invaded Indian lands and fled in haste by jumping off a huge bluff north of Jesup. It is now called Oglethorpe Bluff.

The story of Hannah's Island—located in the dangerous Narrows, where the current runs swiftly—was part of every rafthand's oral legacy. Brainard Cheney summarized the essential details of the haunted place: "A bunch of soldiers camping there during the war had a woman. They all had had her and she died. Her name was Hannah and they called the island after her, because her ghost haunted it." No former pilot or rafthand would admit to having stopped at Hannah's Island, and all told stories of rafthands to whom bad things had happened there. Cheney included one of these episodes in his novel *This Is Adam*.

> That night Adam was tormented in his sleep. He dreamed that he was drifting timber down the Altamaha on high water. It came night, and he couldn't find a place to tie on the mainland, so he tied up his raft to an island in the river. After he had made camp, it came to him that this was Hannah's Island and supposed to be haunted by the ghost of a whore that a company of soldiers did to death during the War. And it seemed that he had no more than realized it when the ghost appeared to him out of the cane brake, naked, the color of a scraped pig, with smoke pouring out of her belly.

Today a few boaters and canoeists know about Hannah, and they pass on much of the rafthands' lore about this lonely spot.

In 1992 Delma Presley spent eight days on a canoe trip with seven members of Rafthands of the Altamaha and Friends Together in Service (RAFTS), formed in 1982. On this particular outing they were retracing a popular raft route of the late 1890s—from Murdock McRae's Landing on the Ocmulgee River to Darien on the coast. After the fifth day on the river, the crew had begun the swift passage through the Narrows. It was a stunningly beautiful day in May. In the early afternoon a member of the party mentioned that the crew was likely to pass Hannah's Island about 3:00 p.m. and would therefore not need to worry about the hazards associated with nightfall there. Presley writes:

> Everyone forgot about the infamous location within minutes. Shortly thereafter storm clouds suddenly darkened the skies. The bad weather swept through the valley. Thunder rumbled through the stand of bald cypress ahead of the crew. Sheets of rain lashed the river's surface. Lightning drove the group to seek shelter under the overhanging branches in a cove. We frantically bailed out our canoes, which had filled almost to the point of submerging.
>
> At the storm's climax came a powerful burst of sound and light on the edge of the land in the middle of the channel. All eyes turned to a giant cypress that bore a fresh gash more than forty feet long. The bark, which had peeled away, seemed to be smoldering. The storm continued unabated for a few minutes more and then died as abruptly as it had begun. Sun broke through the departing clouds. Consulting the rafthands' map of the Altamaha, a crew member sighed. "What the hell would you expect, folks? We're right by Hannah's Island, and she still remembers."

Rafthands plied the Altamaha until the 1900s, when railroads and highways replaced the waterways as favored routes of transportation. Timber companies supported by William E. Dodge, a Wall Street financier, depleted some forests of their original stand of lightwood as early as 1903. In the 1920s rafting was practiced occasionally by a dwindling number of rafthands, and by the 1930s the rafting era in Wiregrass history had ended.

As James Rollison approached his ninth decade in 1972, he looked back on the rafthands he had known. "They were like me," he said. "They were very ignorant. They never went to school, I don't reckon, in their lives, as much as I did. I don't know. But they were a very ignorant type of people. Good people." He remembered the era of the great rafts as a kind of egalitarian universe in which individuals earned status through their skills, regardless of social class. "The best rafthand was master of field and forest, and he knew, really understood, the river." Admonishing his interviewer, Rollison added: "As you go along through life, remember one thing: You never know what kind of heart's beneath a ragged vest. Will you remember that? Keep that in mind."

The river and the people who depended on it have left behind a rich collection of traditions. The culture of the rafthands was conservative in a philosophical sense though not necessarily in a political one. This was the culture of the "Hard Shell" Primitive Baptist Church, where brothers and sisters celebrate the Lord's Supper with real wine and sing hymns the Sacred Harp way, without musical instruments to accompany them.

Rafting was more than a job. It was a way of living, and it reflected core beliefs about humankind and nature. Rafthands believed that we should respect the person who lives close to the earth and who understands the cycles of nature. We should also see ourselves in the broader context of the human community, enriched through cooperative undertakings with distant neighbors and transient colleagues.

CHAPTER 5

The Sacred Harp and Southern Gospel Music

The weekend (from Friday through Sunday) is a time for sacred music. Although much of it is heard in churches, secular spaces are also used for performances. High school auditoriums, city and state parks, county farm centers, fishing and hunting lodges—all serve as arenas for the gospel sound in Wiregrass Country today. Certainly other secular musical forms coexist, but gospel sings, singing conventions, and anniversary concerts represent the more diverse and enduring community-based forms of expression. People can sometimes be heard to say, "That other junk, I never cared for that. I wasn't raised with it. . . . These frolics, juke joints and stuff like that. I never did go for that."

Gospel music here encompasses a wide variety of forms. Southern gospel music includes the traditional, bluegrass, country, African American, new southern, and new southern country styles. Each is performed with nearly the same frequency, sometimes on the stage and even by the same singers. Each group has a style of its own, and the broad tradition of gospel offers something for everyone. The musical forms themselves are quite distinctive genres with social components that reflect the spiritual and Sacred Harp traditions in the South.

The various musical forms, both traditional and commercialized, grew out of the Great Awakening. Much has been written about the camp meetings that swept across New England only to stall in the South. In Brooks County, Georgia, for example, camp meetings were held consecutively until 1881, when it was decided to discontinue them and to build a real church edifice. The meetings typically began on Tuesday and continued until the following Monday. In the beginning, enslaved Africans did the cooking and tended the stock. At daybreak, a trumpet blew to arouse the campers for prayer. A second service took place at eleven, a third at three, and the fourth at "candle lighting." The different services often lasted so long that they merged with each other and became one continuous observance. The laying-by period of late July into October became associated with these annual religious events.

At camp meetings there were usually no hymnbooks for people to use. The preacher initiated a song and was soon joined by the congregation in a call-and-response pattern. The songs relied heavily on choral refrains. Revival spirituals often used the tunes of familiar folk songs. In time, Sacred Harp compositions safeguarded many camp meeting spirituals by incorporating their melodies. The songs thus created became some of the most popular in *The Sacred Harp*. Like the camp meetings, religious revivals, and the music itself, Sacred Harp sings provided a welcome sense of familiarity and belonging and ultimately helped consolidate a way of life.

The songbook *The Sacred Harp*, first published in Philadelphia in 1844 by B. F. White and E. J. King, gave its name to the singing style, but the musical style had earlier origins. The itinerant singing schoolmaster was common in colonial New England, and various masters competed in their efforts to devise an instructional system whereby classes could be taught to sing "by note." By the eighteenth century, religious songbooks were using shape notes to indicate the sounds on the then popular English musical scale fa-sol-la-fa-sol-la-mi-fa. From the fuguing tunes of William Billings to the popular melodies of Jeremiah Ingalls, religious songs found widespread circulation in hymn books such as William Walker's *Southern Harmony*, which was immensely popular throughout the South in the early nineteenth century.

William Law, a New Englander, first introduced shape notes into the singing school tradition during the Great Awakening in the early nineteenth century. The use of differently shaped note heads (a triangle, a circle, a square, and a diamond) to denote the fa, sol, la, and mi musical syllables was an important innovation. As the singing school tradition declined in New England, new shape note songbooks, such as *Kentucky Harmony*, *Virginia Harmony*, and *Union Harmony*, gained widespread popularity in the South. Within this context, *The Sacred Harp* made its initial appearance in 1844 and remained the most popular shape note songbook in its various revisions despite the rapid decline of four-shape tune books in the latter half of the nineteenth century.

Three revisions of *The Sacred Harp* are currently in use. The White revision, published in 1911 by J. L. White, is now used only in a few isolated areas of north Georgia. The most recent revision, the Denson revision, first published in 1935, is by far the most widely used of the *Sacred Harp* revisions. It is found at most Sacred Harp sings throughout Georgia, in north Alabama, and in parts of Mississippi and Tennessee.

Both white and African American singers in south Alabama use the Cooper revision of *The Sacred Harp*, first published in 1902. W. M. Cooper, from Dothan, Alabama, in his edition transposed, or "remodeled," a number of songs into a lower key that could be sung more easily. Cooper also revised the songs by standardizing the alto part in all selections, a significant change that was perpetuated by later revisers. Finally, Cooper added a number of gospel songs and camp meeting selections.

Cooper's inclusion of more contemporary songs in the 1902 revision was at least partly a response to the surge in popularity of seven-shape note music among both whites and African Americans. The seven-syllable character note system of music had been common in the South since the mid-nineteenth century and took on new vitality with a flurry of new publishing activity. Various authors of four-shape songbooks became seven-shape adherents. William Walker, the author of *Southern Harmony*, later published the seven-shape *Christian Harmony*.

The later Denson Sacred Harp revision (1935), most popular in north Alabama, reacted to the more contemporary Cooper revision with a more consciously historical approach, with both old tunes and newer compositions framed in pre-1870 musical styles. Approximately one-third of the 598 songs in the Cooper revision of the Sacred Harp are of the post-1870 gospel style.

The singing conventions chose their own published revisions and for the most part kept to their choices. Within each community, the choice of revision became part of the singing tradition passed along. In the Georgia Wiregrass people chose the seven-note system rather than the four shapes of the Cooper revision. This seven-note form, known as dorayme, differs from the standard system of notation in the shape of the notes alone. Advocates approved of it because the music it set forth was contemporary and permitted musical accompaniment. Songbook sizes (the Cooper revision is oblong, so that each sung part has its own line), instruments, hymn texts, and certain other rudiments differ within these two musical traditions. Their social function, their origin, and their sociocultural dynamic remained the same, however. Dorayme has been described as bridging the distance between the folk spirituals of the nineteenth century, modern sanctified music, and the commercialized sound of Nashville gospel.

Georgia, Alabama, and North Florida remain central to the Sacred Harp musical tradition today. Hugh McGraw, director of the publishing company that prints the popular Denson revision in Bremen, Georgia, says, "It's a dying art. . . . At the turn of the century, there were thousands of Sacred Harp singers in Georgia alone. Today, there are, at the most, 4,000 to 5,000 fa-sol-la singers left in America. We aim to preserve it." The book, the schools, and the people have all been viewed as contributing to the

Dewey Williams and Japheth Jackson conduct a singing school in Ozark, Alabama, in February 1989. Photo by Joey Brackner. Courtesy of the Alabama State Council on the Arts, Montgomery.

tradition's longevity. In toto, southern composers compiled about forty-two books.

Camp meetings and singing conventions, significant social events, helped to combat the isolation and loneliness of southern life. In the rural setting, singing schools represented a major community activity. Until recently, area newspapers published lists of people who attended. People spent days learning how to sight-read shape note music and how to lead a song. Even today, devotees often speak of having been "born into the tradition" or of having "learned it with their alphabets." When shape note singing was at the height of its popularity, excursion trains brought between 3,000 and 5,000 people to sites such as the Royal Singing Convention in Mystic, Irwin County, Georgia.

With the introduction of singing schools, American music took on an increasingly secular quality that has encompassed sacred music as well as popular. As sacred songs were being sung, other social functions were being fulfilled. The social activities often resembled those at secular events like a circus or a fair. The annual convention became an occasion for reminiscences. According to folklorist Dave Stanley, "Back then, say those who remember, young men observed the girls in their 'convention dresses,' or courted under the trees; others would sneak off to the woods for a drink.

There were fights and children's games, politicians looking forward to fall elections worked the crowds, and funeral homes distributed fans with a patriotic scene or landscape on one side, advertising on the other, while concessioners sold ice cream and soft drinks." Despite the distractions, few lost sight of the true reason for attending, which was both religious and performative. A recent practitioner commented: "At a singing I heard someone ma[k]e a beautiful and moving statement. He said in part, 'Sacred Harp Singers love one another. They love each other better than they do in the churches a lot of the time and this is one of the things that makes Sacred Harp singing love on and on.' "

Sacred Harp singing conventions were nondenominational. A few denominations, however, like the Primitive Baptist and Church of Christ, find Sacred Harp singing congenial. These churches frown on musical instruments, preferring a cappella song for scriptural reasons. Ralph Stanley, a bluegrass artist, grew up in the Primitive Baptist Church. He said, "That's the kind of church I was raised in. They don't use any kind of music (instruments)—we just sang without any kind of music. If ya pitch 'em too high, they'll stop an' start over, till they get 'em right." The Church of Christ notes that in the Old Testament, David, not God, proclaimed, "Make a joyful noise unto the Lord" (Psalm 66:1), and the church therefore conducts its religious services too without instrumental accompaniment. Some elders still lead the hymns by marking time as in the Sacred Harp tradition. One elder acknowledged a lack of familiarity with "round notes" (standard notation) and relied on memorization—another trace of the shape note tradition. The music that we now consider traditional gospel was actually composed and standardized a hundred years ago, but over time it entered the public domain as part of the oral tradition. Songs that bear the traditional gospel stamp include hymns like "Leaning on the Everlasting Arm," "Bringing in the Sheaves," "How Great Thou Art," and especially "Amazing Grace."

The Cooper revision of *The Sacred Harp* continues to be the primary book for African American and white Sacred Harp singers in southeast Alabama. In recent years, however, a variant first published in Ozark, Alabama, in 1934 has become increasingly popular. *The Colored Sacred Harp* contains seventy-seven songs, all but one composed by African American singers from southeast Alabama and northwest Florida. Southeast Alabama has enjoyed a vibrant and rare African American Sacred Harp tradition for well over a century. The Henry County, Alabama, Sacred Harp Singing Convention celebrated its one hundredth anniversary in 1980. Although historical proof is lacking, enslaved Africans may well have sung Sacred Harp with southeast Alabama whites as early as the 1850s, establishing segregated conventions and sings after the Civil War. No area of the pres-

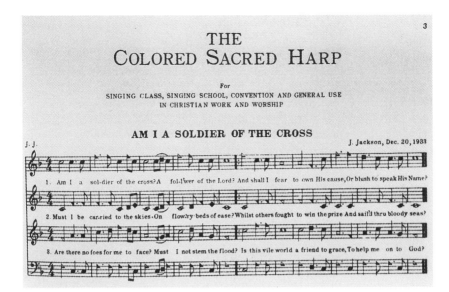

A page from *The Colored Sacred Harp.* Photo courtesy of the Alabama Center for Traditional Culture, Montgomery.

ent-day United States rivals southeast Alabama in the volume of organized African American Sacred Harp singing activity.

The Colored Sacred Harp listed Judge Jackson (1883–1958) as its author and publisher. Jackson and members of his family provided twenty-seven of the book's compositions. Methodist preacher H. Webster Woods, a student of Judge Jackson, composed fourteen songs. Judge Jackson had first heard Sacred Harp singing as a teenager in Montgomery County, Alabama, and was composing tunes of his own by his twenty-fifth birthday. In the 1920s, Jackson had several of his compositions printed on broadsheets, which he gave and sold to friends and acquaintances throughout Dale County.

In the 1930s, a committee of the Dale County Colored Musical Institute and the Alabama and Florida Union State Convention made recommendations for a new four-shape songbook. The venture received a powerful endorsement from these two groups. The Alabama and Florida Union State Convention, founded in 1922, is the highest organizational unit in the region's African American Sacred Harp community, the convention to which all the county conventions now belong. The now-defunct Dale County Colored Musical Institute played an important role in the late 1920s and 1930s.

J. JACKSON, OZARK, ALA.
Author of The Colored Sacred Harp
1931

Judge Jackson, Ozark, Alabama, c. 1931. Photo courtesy of the Alabama Center for Traditional Culture, Montgomery.

According to Japheth Jackson, Judge Jackson's son, "The convention voted it wanted to have a school where *our* children would learn how to write music, not just read it." The Dale County Colored Musical Institute may have been created in response to publication of the Cooper *Sacred Harp*, published in 1927. Judge Jackson had submitted compositions to the all-white committee in charge of revising the Cooper *Sacred Harp*. They were rejected. Judge Jackson may have decided to publish *The Colored Sacred Harp* as early as 1927. The following text appears in the front of the book:

> We, the Committee appointed by the Dale County Colored Musical Institute and the Alabama and Florida Union State Convention offer the following recommendations: First: That we will have a musical book. Second: That the name of the book will be The Colored Sacred Harp. Third: That four shaped notes be used. Fourth: That Bro. Jackson be the author of the book. We hope this little book may prove a great blessing and be the means of saving souls.

The committee report was signed by fifteen members, many representing families still prominent in the African American Sacred Harp tradition.

It is difficult to know exactly what prompted the publication of *The Col-*

ored Sacred Harp. New, original composition has always been a part of the Sacred Harp tradition. The numerous twentieth-century revisions of the Cooper and Denson Sacred Harp books attest to this fact. African Americans in southeast Alabama are believed to have assisted whites in the composition of four-shape songs. We also know that Judge Jackson composed songs as early as 1904 and that H. Webster Woods and W. E. Glanton (then president of the Alabama and Florida Union State Convention) were composing music by the 1920s.

In the depression year of 1934, Jackson himself was obliged to provide the primary financial backing for the publication. Bascom F. Faust, a white banker from Ozark and an important figure in the Sacred Harp community of southeast Alabama, provided an additional $1,000. Perhaps for this reason, he is the only white composer with a song in *The Colored Sacred Harp* ("Eternal Truth Thy Word"). Otherwise the book was clearly the product of the collaborative efforts of southeast Alabama's African American Sacred Harp community. A total of twenty-six composers were represented, but Judge Jackson had the largest hand.

The Colored Sacred Harp is an important historical document that illustrates the musical life of this Sacred Harp singing community. When it first appeared in 1934, African American shape note singing was at its height in southeast Alabama. Japheth Jackson remembers that 1,000 copies of the book were printed. "A firm in Chicago did the printing. I went with my dad in a mule-drawn wagon to pick up the books at the Ozark train station." For a variety of reasons, however, *The Colored Sacred Harp* was not readily adopted by the African American community and nearly disappeared from the community's active repertoire before its first reprinting in 1973.

One reason for the book's initial failure to be accepted had to do with timing. It was published during the worst of the depression, when cash was scarce among African Americans in southeast Alabama. Also, the Sacred Harp community is conservative and slow to add new songs to its repertoire. Finally, jealousy and resentment of Judge Jackson's role in the publication caused it to be shunned, especially by singers outside Dale County.

Jackson had apparently promised the contributing composers that they would receive some financial compensation after the book came out. When the moment came, however, Jackson, who had already invested much of his own money in the project, decided to wait until the book showed a profit. At the time, Jackson was president of the Dale County Singing Convention and was running for president of the state convention. He was ultimately defeated in part because of controversy surrounding the book.

Still, although *The Colored Sacred Harp* was not totally accepted by the African American community, it was never completely rejected. The Judge Jackson honorary sing was established in 1935. Then, and in subsequent anniversary sings (on the third Sunday in April), participants set aside periods for singing from *The Colored Sacred Harp*.

Ironically, in the 1990s, with a steadily decreasing number of active African American Sacred Harp singers, *The Colored Sacred Harp* is enjoying its greatest popularity to date. Scholars and the African American community have rediscovered the book simultaneously. It has been reprinted three times since 1973. Old jealousies and resentments have disappeared with the passing of the older singers. The current generation appreciates the book's historical significance. With the gradual waning of the singing tradition, *The Colored Sacred Harp* has become a source of pride among members of Alabama's African American shape note singing community.

On almost any Sunday between March and October, when the weather permits travel and dinners outdoors, Sacred Harp devotees join with fellow singers at County Line Church in Slocomb or the Mount Sinai Church in Henry County or at any one of a dozen or so churches in the southeastern Alabama counties of Barbour, Coffee, Dale, Geneva, Henry, Houston, and Pike. There they form the square and sing fa-sol-la. Today about fifteen African American Sacred Harp sings occur annually in the Wiregrass region of southeast Alabama. Half are convention sings and the other half honorary sings.

After the Civil War, in the wake of the large conventions, a number of county conventions began to spring up, and African American singers followed this practice. Today there are four African American county conventions (Barbour, Dale, Henry, and Pike) and the state convention (Alabama and Florida Union Singing Convention) to which all the county conventions send official delegates. The convention meetings last one or two days. Various announcements and committee reports are interspersed throughout the singing.

Most honorary sings began as tributes to singers during their lifetimes and continued as memorials after their deaths. Honorary or memorial sings always last one day (a Sunday). They begin at about eleven, break for dinner at one, and continue until about four or four-thirty. Apart from a speech honoring the individual in question, the singing is not interrupted by any reports or business.

Besides convention and honorary sings, there were at one time holiday sings. A May Day sing, commemorating Emancipation Day, which in southeast Alabama is celebrated on May 28, began in 1910 and died out in the 1970s. An effort to revive the May Day sing in the early 1990s did not succeed, perhaps for lack of an organizing structure.

At any sing the president and the tuner play key roles. The president must keep the sing moving, call on song leaders, and act as a sort of master of ceremonies throughout the event. The tuner, traditionally the most skilled male singer, is responsible for setting the tonic chord, or "chording" the song. The key chosen often bears no relation to the key printed in the book. Instead, songs are often pitched higher or lower for the comfort of most of the singers. Often the tuner helps weaker or less experienced song leaders by singing extra loud and using broad arm gestures to mark the time and tempo.

Several singing schools are held in the summer. These used to be all-day sessions running five days a week for two weeks. In the 1990s they are more typically one-week evenings-only programs. The singing school teacher spends most of class time reviewing the rudiments of music printed in the Sacred Harp book, practicing both major and minor scales, and teaching students how to mark time and lead songs. Singers of varying skills attend, from the young beginner to the experienced older singer. This mixing together of skill levels provides an opportunity for the beginner to learn as much through observation and imitation as through formal rote learning and recitation.

On the day of a typical black Sacred Harp sing, the singers arrive in the late morning and seat themselves in the square according to voice part, the basses facing the trebles and the tenors facing the altos. Every singer is invited to lead a song. When called upon, the song leader comes to the middle of the square, calls out the page number, and waits for the tuner to chord the song. Song leaders avoid repeating a song that has already been sung, or "used." They may not do so, however, if the song leader is particularly old or young or if a song has special significance for the individual (having been, perhaps, the favorite song of a recently deceased relative).

Once the tuner has chorded the song, the song leader, standing in the middle of the square, facing the tenor section, leads the singers first through the notes to the song and then through the lyrics. This practice reflects procedure in the traditional singing school classes, where singers are taught to sing first the notes and then the words. This singing of the notes gives Sacred Harp music its most distinctive sound, as four parts of harmony are simultaneously vocalized by the singers. This singing of the notes, too, has led many to call Sacred Harp "fa-sol-la" singing.

Sacred Harp is a democratic and participatory musical tradition. It gives every singer an opportunity to lead a song. Often, older or infirm singers will ask younger singers to lead. The motions of the most accomplished singers are often highly stylized and generally convey more emotion than the motions of white Sacred Harp song leaders. Young children are taught in singing school to mark time with their right arm while holding the book in their left. Typically a song leader will stand in place at the center of the square while leading the note singing. When African American singers begin to lead the lyrics portion of the song, they often "walk time," rhythmically pacing from one side of the square to the other and taking care never to turn their backs on the tenor section. The more confident song leaders proudly display their distinctive conducting styles. During fuguing songs in particular, the leader might gesture to each section of the square as it adds its part. On occasion a song leader may elicit applause or some other emotional response from the group. Sometimes a singer "falls out," overwhelmed by spiritual emotion. At such times the affected individual may offer personal testimony, followed by a repetition of the song's last verse or refrain.

Sacred Harp singing, with both white and African American singers, is primarily an activity for older adults. Although children are typically trained early in its rudiments, they often abandon the tradition in their late teens or childrearing years, returning to the tradition in late middle age. With the increased mobility of modern life, and the concomitant disruption of the traditional extended family, the number of active singers has dropped, and those who remain tend to be considerably older than they were a generation ago. The two most active leaders have been Dewey Williams and Japheth Jackson, who is over seventy years old; Dewey Williams, who received a National Heritage Award for his contributions to the tradition, passed away after his honorary ninety-seventh birthday celebration and sing. There is a very real concern that the tradition may not survive into the twenty-first century.

Southern gospel has continued to develop a life of its own, becoming commercialized as a popular form of American music. By the 1960s, bluegrass music emerged as an independent entity. Bluegrass originated in Appalachia as country music that uses a string band and is acoustical in style. The string instruments generally include the five-string banjo, acoustic guitar, and fiddle or mandolin. Although the songs are contemporary and have been formally composed, most are considered traditional and conform to other Anglo-American ballad and folksong styles. Bluegrass bands frequently use traditional gospel songs to begin and end a concert. Now many bluegrass gospel bands exist and play exclusively sacred music and usually do so in secular spaces.

Country gospel, which, like the bluegrass variety, draws upon and closely follows secular country music, is probably the most representative form of southern gospel music in Wiregrass Country. Country gospel tends to be lower in pitch, with a slower average tempo than most bluegrass music. Although the sound of country gospel comes from Nashville, it holds great significance for performers in the Wiregrass.

African American music is widely believed to have influenced the country music tradition. The musician "Pappy" Neal McCormick, who comes from DeFuniak Springs and received the Florida Heritage Award, is a case

A night gospel sing at Mount Pleasant Baptist Church in Vada, Georgia, c. 1977.
Photo by Paul Kwilecki. Reproduced by permission.

in point and also something of an icon within the region. He is credited
with having given Hank Williams his first regular job. In the 1920s McCormick learned to play the steel guitar from an African American laborer at
a local sawmill. His blues-style guitar, like that of many other country singers, clearly displays an African American influence. In addition, many
country songs rely heavily on tunes canonized by the African American
gospel tradition. Then, too, after the 1940s, country gospel quartets borrowed from black gospel quartets as both gained in popularity.

Harmony is an important dimension of country gospel music. Traditionally, gospel quartets borrowed the close harmonic triads of the barbershop
quartet. Singers also learned to harmonize at shape note singing schools,
where quartets were formed for practice. The predominantly male acts involved four-part harmony that required a phenomenal bass, an entrancing
alto, a mello baritone, and a penetrating tenor. In the African American
quartet tradition, the high tenor part, as a hallmark, will shift into a falsetto
voice. The audience, expecting it to do so, responds approvingly. The high
tenor often sings the lead in country gospel music as well. When he sings
the high notes, however, his part may be used humorously. Today more
ensembles are emerging, to the detriment of quartets in both musical traditions.

As Bill Monroe is considered the father of bluegrass, Thomas Dorsey is considered the father of African American gospel music. When he performed publicly with Ma Rainey and others, Dorsey was known as Barrelhouse Tom and Georgia Tom. By 1930, this onetime itinerant blues performer and composer was a prolific gospel music composer and promoter. Because he invented what is now known as the Chicago School of Music, scholars link the music exclusively with the urban experience. Dorsey's music, however, transformed the musical appreciation, repertoire, and traditions of African American rural church members and religious leaders, who tuned their radios to Nashville, especially at night, and liked what they heard. His musical influence on the rural South was profound.

Over the decades, African American gospel has undergone numerous changes. It has been described perhaps most aptly, however, by Tony Heilbut, who called it "good news and bad times." The form evolved during the depression years as the music of spiritual uplift. In practice, African American gospel builds on every musical tradition intercepted or created by African people in America. Tommie Gabriel, a local impresario, draws attention to its evangelical function: "Maybe we can get them all [converts] by singing different songs." The songs sung today often cross over subgeneric lines and echo the past. From spirituals to standard Baptist hymns, all have been gospelized—endowed with refrains and syncopated rhythms that evoke the shout. These hallmarks of popular expression, it has been suggested, carry the most emotional weight.

New southern gospel, another contemporary form, in its composition imitates traditional gospel. The compositions often take the form of a ballad narrating biblical events. Sometimes the singer performs accompanied by a prerecorded sound track. The high-tech sound supports the dramatic narrative content and creates an emotionally charged atmosphere. The fully orchestrated background is replete with special effects. This type of performance minimizes the role of musicians and frees the singer to develop an individual presentation style. Sound tracks—a part of this genre accepted by professionals and amateurs alike—have the drawback that, being prerecorded, they do not allow for spontaneity in performance.

New southern country gospel, finally, can be described as having been inspired by rock music. More experimental than the other forms, it breaks with the southern white tradition by boldly adopting a contemporary secular tone. The use of percussive drum within the sacred format is the newest innovation. Critics of this subgenre often charge that it sacrifices spiritual song lyrics for the sake of a big sound.

In several African American communities, singing conventions have begun performing songs in the African American gospel tradition. In Georgia, the Thomas-Grady County Singing Convention dates back to 1929, beginning in the dorayme tradition. By 1949, the convention had transformed itself by introducing African American gospel music. The president began attending the National Baptist Singing Conventions sponsored by Thomas Dorsey. The county convention convenes every two months on the Friday before the third Sunday. The detailed, prearranged schedules are set so that they mirror countless African American social events. No dates can be assigned for an activity with a sacred component until the pastoral days of neighboring churches have been taken into account.

Another convention, the Georgia-Florida Singing Union, has met consecutively since 1953 only on fifth Sundays. Since churches met only once a month, the fifth Sunday was traditionally a wild card. As one preacher's wife observed, "Congregation thought that there was only one Sunday in the month. Eventually, they learned that there is a fifth Sunday too." These Sundays have become traditional and constitute special dates on many religious calendars for union meetings, singing conventions, and so on. The Georgia-Florida Singing Union consists of eight churches in Georgia and three in Florida, since participation in Florida has been waning.

At the contemporary singing conventions, choral music predominates. The format is basically the same as that followed in the shape note tradition, but the program provides for the various choral groups to perform in sequence rather than for different individuals to lead the assembled singers. Despite the shift in musical interests, the structure of the past is evident in the program.

Convention sites rotate in accordance with an arrangement prescribed decades ago. Each choir hosts a singing convention at fixed intervals, usually within three years. Like singing conventions in the past, these events usually do not include any religious sermons. Lay organizers prepare introductory and closing remarks, discuss financial business, and make announcements. As in the past, the gatherings remain tangential to the activities associated with the various African American churches.

Singing conventions historically offered a banner to the class that sang best at the annual gathering. At today's African American singing conventions, organizers continue to use banners to inspire friendly competition. Nowadays, however, the banner goes to the choir that collects the most dues from its membership. As part of the tradition, supporters purchase a badge (a colored ribbon) to identify the choir of their choice and to help that choir win. These customs have helped preserve rural African American churches. Tommie Gabriel, president of the Thomas-Grady County Singing Convention, spoke of the furnishings that the rural churches had financed through their collective endeavor:

> That has fixed it where we got kitchens. The same conventions got kitchen, air conditions. Some of the only air conditions that they would ever have is

A rural church near Iron City, c. 1985. Photo by Paul Kwilecki. Reproduced by permission.

from these choirs, that money like they're raising. Kitchens, air conditions, rugs on the floor, all that seating that they got—comfortable. The church couldn't do that ordinarily with a one or two Sunday church. Each convention, the whole church comes in together, and they put on little affairs leading up to it so that when that day comes that will be a big general rally. Say, a union meeting and association meeting should come to your church and pay off all those deacons, there is no money left at those churches. That's the only thing that we have where money's raised to help the church is singing.

The conventions often raise more than $1,000 each session for the host choir.

The close relationship that once existed between singing conventions and many small community churches is becoming strained, however. Ministers who are unfamiliar with the tradition (and, as previously noted, ministers were never an integral part of it) dislike being secondary. Some white adherents of the Sacred Harp are increasingly criticized for impeding progress. African American Sacred Harp singers are more and more constrained because their small conventions fail to produce adequate revenue. When there is a conflict over dates, local churches renege on the Sacred Harp singing conventions, since another event will usually raise more money. The African American singing conventions that have evolved with the

Mt. Zion AME Church with Sunday School class on steps, 1981. Photo by Paul Kwilecki. Reproduced by permission.

times and sing African American gospel music encounter the least resistance and attract a more youthful following.

For most white residents of Wiregrass Country, too, the gospel sing has replaced the Sacred Harp tradition. Musical performances feature more professional artists in a concert setting. In the dorayme shape note tradition, spotlighted performers were the "specials": solos, duets, trios, quartets, family groups, and piano or organ instrumentals. Publishing companies competed for buyers and hired quartets to promote their books at conventions.

Stanley Smith, a white Sacred Harp enthusiast, contrasted the modern gospel sings with the traditional singing conventions: "People like to be entertained. They don't like to participate. They'd rather pay money and sit there and be sung to than get in there and take part with it. They're good. I like to hear them a little bit, but if I can't pretty soon get in there and sing with them, I don't have any use for them." Unlike this tradition bearer, many Sacred Harp singers have moved from the square back into the pews.

According to folklorist Charles Wolfe, white southern gospel "underwent in a few years a complete revolution, and moved from being a publisher-dominated music to an artist-dominated music." A gospel sing may feature big-name professionals, semiprofessionals, and amateur performers alike. In Wiregrass Country the all-night sing has a long history. Bonifray, Florida ("the home of the largest all-night singing in the world"), and Waycross, Georgia, are renowned regionally for events that fill football stadiums and convention centers year after year. In most cases, local churches host concerts at regular intervals that spotlight a single act. The themes are those of gospel music generally: individual salvation, daily suffering, hearth and home, grief for the deceased, and the good Christian's duty to take action. At these musical events, the evangelical focus makes the lyrics more prominent.

Travel is an important part of the gospel musical inheritance in this region. According to one Sacred Harp enthusiast, supporters of gospel "must drive an average of nearly 300 miles round-trip to attend their singings and that's in pleasant weather. I have attended two to three a month, shows how much they have meant to me." Once the singers, musicians, and supporters of southern gospel music have become part of a network, travel becomes a compulsion. The musical tradition, which extends beyond the tristate Wiregrass area, thus helps bind people within the religious and social order.

Enthusiasts declare, "Southern gospel is not a single sound; it's a single message." Tommie Gabriel put the matter a little differently: "Each song ought to be able to tell a story within itself. If it doesn't have any meaning, then it isn't worth singing."

CHAPTER 6

Storytellers and Their Tales

Wiregrass storytellers eagerly recite historical legends, supernatural tales, Bible-based stories, and personal experience narratives, as illustrated by the life history interviews conducted throughout the region. Recurrent motifs reflect a core of shared social, economic, and cultural experiences.

The everyday narratives of Wiregrass Country exhibit distinctive beliefs, customs, and practices. Despite the significant changes of the past century, from new technologies to racial integration, people retain knowledge that reflects their historical and cultural past. As a part of their subliminal regional identity, area residents also learn to appreciate the supernatural. Both aspects surface in narratives on everything from the art of working mules to the art of locating buried treasures. Each narrative embodies its own profound truth.

Southern violence looms large in folk narratives of the region. County histories routinely preserve historical legends and imbue them with community values and norms. These histories habitually comment, for example, on the local prevalence of violence. Some blame outside influences and speak of the peaceful, idyllic community that existed before outsiders came to work in the lumber industry: "Native South Georgians, therefore, began carrying pistols for protection; in fact, weapons were a part of the costumes. N. L. Turner, who was one of the best informed of the old settlers, said that he could identify his friends by the sound of their pistols as we identify now by the honk of automobile horns. Men carried pistols to town, parties, and to church." Sawmill and turpentine camps created an atmosphere of random, unpredictable danger. Violence, however, had long been endemic to the South of which the Wiregrass is a part.

In the words of a recent community-based folk drama, "If you are killed in the South, you probably know your attacker." As on any frontier, a general rowdiness characterized leisure activities. According to Fred Watson, a local historian in Wiregrass Alabama, "Drunkenness, shootings, knife and fist fights were common occurrences in the little town, especially on Saturdays when the farmers and turpentine workers came into town to swap tales, whittle on the town well frame, patronize the saloons, and buy supplies." At least initially, hostile people targeted others of the same race, sex, and even family rather than members of different social and economic groups.

Many written descriptions of the Wiregrass as recently as the early twentieth century fit our stereotypes of life in the Old West. The following editorial, published in 1913 and rediscovered by Alabama historian Val McGee, endorsed capital punishment as a possible deterrent: "Something must be done in Dale County to stop so much murder. Within the past two months four people have been killed besides a number of other serious offenses committed. There was a time when Dale County had the reputation of hanging people, when they took humanlife, and the laws were observed, and few killings occurred. Something must be done in this county to stop this wholesale lawlessness, and a few hangings occasionally, as we had in the good old days, might help some."

Many Wiregrass communities earned a reputation as "tough towns." Public opinion sometimes blamed whiskey. According to one victim, "They would drink wild rum out of town and come in here and load up on good whiskey. . . . That would run them crazy and they were not used to any law. Naturally, when they were taught there must be law here, plenty of trouble followed."

Southern violence escalated with growing racial animosity as more African Americans and other indigent workers entered the region. Wayne Flynt described the problem: "When poor whites became frustrated and dissatisfied, they often directed their anger at blacks. Usually a threat to poor white status was the catalyst to disorder. Black tenants replaced whites. Or black strikebreakers entered mines to assume jobs previously held by free black and white miners. Blacks ran for public office or in other ways became 'uppity.' Or most threatening of all, blacks infringed on the sexual realm." Reconstruction-era social change aroused fear, and the area's white settlers struggled vainly to restore the antebellum social order.

Interestingly, county historians often bypass scenes or sites of racial violence without comment, as if they were nothing out of the ordinary. One story, for example, tells how men "kidnapped" an impounded railroad locomotive in 1899 to guarantee their town's progress. "Leaving Dothan at sunset, the crowd stopped at Newton for refreshments and to examine a 'haunted tree' from which a Negro had been hanged during reconstruction days."

At any rate, more whites than African Americans were lynched in the Wiregrass before the 1870s. Fred Watson provides one account:

> On Dec. 3, 1864, a good man by the name of Bill Skeeto was hanged to the limb of a post oak near the foot of the bridge on the west side of the Choctawhatchee River at Newton by Captain Brear's Home Guards. The limb stood out towards the south and was so low that when the buggy was pulled from under the doomed man his feet touched the ground while he was struggling with the last enemy of man.
>
> George Echols took his crutch and dug a hole under his feet so they would hang clear. From that day until now that hole in the ground has been cleaned out by some strange hand, seen or unseen, and thousands have personally noted this strange phenomenon. . . .
>
> Many people have told that they had filled this hole with trash many times and returned to find it empty. In 1871 the late Thomas Fain built a bridge there. When it washed away, John Knight was employed to build another to take its place. . . . They pitched their camp under the oak tree to which Skeeto was hanged. . . . They watched the hole in the ground with zealous eyes, and they say it was filled up every night. One morning after they had pitched their camp they got up to find the hole left clean. . . .
>
> The story goes that when he was nearing his doom and the rope was around his neck, he was asked if he had anything to say. He told them [his murderers] that he would like to pray. Thinking that he wanted to pray for himself, the wish was granted, but he prayed for his murderers. This so stung them that they quickly threw the rope over the limb and pushed the buggy from under him. He died, hanging from the limb of the tree, without having finished his prayer.

Such folk legends invariably carry a coda for closure and to communicate prevailing moral values. Accounts of violent deeds typically conclude, as here, with evidence of fascination, a sense of mystery, and moral discomfort with the violence involved.

E. W. Carswell recently explained the importance of reporting such events: "I hate to have to use this sort of thing. But I felt I wanted somebody to see. If I didn't tell it people would wonder after while if it happened. This particular fellow was hung. They thought that he was a deserter from the army. . . . There were six fellows involved and lightning got one, and another died in a swamp. My grandpa thought that they were given medicine for punishment." Carswell may be commenting on the unredemptive value of the rough justice inflicted to uphold "southern honor." According to Bertram Wyatt-Brown, honor, rather than conscience, shame, or guilt, undergirded southern culture. The codas attached to the tales in county histories reflect attempts to resolve these conflicting elements, a goal that is sometimes achieved today by attributing the outcome to divine providence.

The supernatural figures prominently in personal experience narratives for reasons perhaps related to the legacy of violence. The stories also express Southerners' general reverence for the dead. Motorists respectfully stop alongside the road while a funeral cortege is passing by. Many individuals anticipate seeing their loved ones, neighbors, and complete strangers after they die.

Although they are sometimes criticized as superstitious, many Southerners regard the universe as a spiritual arena. The Swedish scholar C. W. von Sydow once observed, "Belief in the existence of spirits is founded not upon loose speculation, but upon concrete, personal experiences, the reality of which is reinforced by sensory perception." Prose narratives that embody the supernatural, then, should be recognized as a subgenre of folktales, the memorate.

Memorates are personal experience narratives of the supernatural told as fact. In *Tall Betsy and Dunce Baby*, Wiregrass Georgia folklorist Mariella Hartsfield recorded one memorate from William Robert Glenn. Glenn's narrative is secondhand but believed to be true:

> Well now, this came from my mama and daddy. They knew Mr. Rit Hayes well. He didn't live very far from where my daddy lived. And everybody knew that Mr. Rit Hayes could see ghosts, or he said he could. . . . there was different things told on him, but my daddy said this happened on a Saturday night—he said very seldom Mr. Hayes would be caught off after dark, he just wouldn't. And he rode on horseback up to Pelham, Georgia—at that time Pelham was a small place. Something happened, and he was detained, and it was afternight. And Papa said they heard a horse coming down the road just as hard as that horse could run. So, Papa's mama—that was Grandma Glenn—said, "Gus, you and Jerry better go outside; I know who that is coming, and more than likely he's gonna stop here—that's Mr. Hayes. And if he does, ya'll take the horse and go on and put him in the lot." Said sure-nuff that horse got right in front of the gate; Mr. Hayes said, "whoa!" pulled back, you know, and stopped that horse so quick. And he said Mr. Hayes just threw them the bridle reins, and he ran right on in the house. So he said him and his brother put the horse in the lot, and they came in, and Mr. Hayes told them there was a woman riding back of the saddle with him. Now, Mr. Rit Hayes's wife died several years before that, and he lived by himself; but he could see her on occasions. And she was riding in the saddle back of him. And they said he wouldn't even go home that night. He spent the night there at the house.

Certain motifs recur in Wiregrass Country memorates. Perilous nocturnal journeys are one. As Hartsfield has accurately noted: "Even in Grady County tales the dead supposedly do return, and if they do not visibly return, many a story is built around the fear that they will do so. The ghosts in the tales collected here do not seem to be terribly vindictive but seem instead to delight in lurking around derelict buildings to frighten travelers."

Another recurrent common motif concerns the perils of staying away from home overnight. A retired African American undertaker, Fred Smith of Cairo, Georgia, provided the following memorate:

> I woke up and I saw look like a cat sitting in the window. I wasn't thinking about no ghosts or nothing. Because see that thing jumped and right straddled me, and he rode me until he got tired and he jumped off. And when he jumped off, he looked like a speckled-face lady. So I told Miss Johnson about it. She said, "my aunt died in that room and I was intending to tell you. Several people have slept in there and said that they saw something." She said, "she was a speckled lady." So, it never bothered me no more; and I never see it no more, but I slept in another room.

Smith's tale combines the ghost and witch motifs. Witches in the African American oral tradition often spend the night riding their victims. The cat witch is still another prevalent motif.

Certain people—but only a few—are clairvoyant. Fred Smith affirmed this belief: "My mother told me that my older brother, what died in Savannah—said, he could see ghosts. When he was a little boy, he would run all between her legs saying a man was riding a toad frog and things like that. And she said that she believed that he could see ghosts. She couldn't see them, but she said that he could see them." Smith's account suggests a kind of second sight that might be associated with other special skills, such as the ability to conjure. A person with these gifts may be called a root doctor, a two-head, and a two-facer.

In contrast, some memorates conclude with rational resolutions. E. W. Carswell presented one example:

> I remember this was so real about a ghost. . . . We had a flu epidemic in 1918–19, and my mother went with me over to near this old house that had been abandoned. People died there from the flu and moved away. We, as neighbors, sort of see after their property some. They had moved away, the survivors were Johnson or something. It was just sitting there and had never been painted in the first place. It was a ghostly looking place. Some people had already been talking about it being haunted. And my mother said, "let's go home." And she got my father. We told my father about it, and he went to see what was bumping around in there. And they were swearing that there have been some ghost stories, and they must have been true. He went in there and checked at it and it was barn owls in there. And they are very ghostly looking things. So we weren't afraid of that particular ghost anymore.

Owls are stock figures in ghostly lore, being familiar from the rational, known world and at the same time connected with supernatural forces. Ambiguous presences, they serve local storytellers well.

Owls appear as culprits in many personal narratives. In the highly symbolic world of folk beliefs, the bird's hoot foretold death. Owls' association with night made them seem particularly macabre. Fred Smith narrated the following incident:

> Let me tell you something funny now. My wife's grandmother died, that was long years ago; and they lived in Alabama. Anyway, she died and I was supposed to take the body over there. I left here that night. And I got another fellow to go with me. And we took it in a truck. (I had a new Buick; I drove it to carry the family there. So that night, nobody went, but the family was in Alabama.) A fellow told me when I get there to go in there and ring the bell and he would come. So I got to the church and went in there. I could see a big lamp sitting back there. They didn't have no lights in the church. And . . . I shined the flashlight. I had Sam _____, (he's still living) and I told him to ring the bell. When he started ringing that bell, he [the caretaker] would come light the lamp and everything and get us. So while he was ringing the bell, the old hoot owl flew down out the steeple and come up to the front where we . . . We had come all the way through the church. But that devilish thing, when he came and we saw those big old eyes, Sam liked to tore up that hallway coming up. He [the caretaker] come on up there after he heard the bell ring. And . . . he told us about that old owl up there. But see they should have told us before we got there, and we would have been looking for an owl in the church. He said they [owls] run him out lots time. But they [the congregation] didn't think nothing about it because it probably would be in the morning when they go. But when we got there at about 12 o'clock at night, with it being dark and a big cemetery on the right hand side of the church, I thought the devil had come with all of his Christian souls.

Humor often relieves the tension in tales of the supernatural. The laughter dispels fear and signals the return of order and predictability.

Other motifs and tale types frequently surfaced during the interviewing process. When allowed to direct their comments conversationally, narrators, such as Tommie Gabriel and Doris Lewis, routinely turned to Bible-based stories in order to make a point. The story of Moses seemed to inform the text most often told by African Americans:

> So, he [Pharaoh] sent out chariots with three men to the chariot. And they had and I mean . . . I don't know how many chariots they say he sent out. But he sent out all that he had, the heaviest chariots he had. So that it would be two men that could deal with them and a driver.

Now, these people weren't even armed but he was just so mad that he just sent them out there to get them. He didn't care what way. Kill them. It didn't make no matter. They weren't going to get away from him. And Moses walking along leading. They almost got to him but . . . the dust from the chariot—round and round—and they covered these people over all night long, all day. They were out there running around trying to find them. The dust from the chariot swept over them and they couldn't find them.

Instead of Moses going up in the mountains where the chariots couldn't go, they said that he was doing the craziest thing that they have ever seen a man do—walking along the seashore. They couldn't understand it. But Moses was watching the clouds. And so he had to follow that what was leading him. And so now, the people were fussing and raising sand: "It would have been better to have stayed down in Egypt and died down there than to get lost out here."

So you see why he had to rely on the Lord guiding him quite often. He [God] told him to stretch out your rod across the sea. And while these people [the army] were still back there in the fog and the dark from the clouds and all that dust, Moses went on cross. Then, when it cleared up and they saw him over there, they went after him. Too late, that thing closed back up on them. That goes to show you that a-l-l through life the Lord has taken care of his people.

Another version, featuring the same biblical figure, illustrates the role religious legends play within the African American socialization process:

The Lord taught us to teach our young the old things. You know? Remember when . . . Now, I taught Bible school last week. I am going to give them all their certificates Sunday at church. You know and everything. So, I talked about Moses and the trip he made from his birth and on down to bringing the children out of Israel. And I was telling them, I said: "Now, when Moses was crossing the Red Sea he told each head of each . . . tribe to get a rock, a stone out there." And you can read it in the Bible. It in there. "Get a stone out of the middle of this sea" that they are crossing. "Take it to the other side of the ocean. Now pile all of those stones together." He said, "in days to come your children will ask you why these stones." And he said, "you can tell them this was the crossing of the Red Sea." This was bringing God's children home. Bringing them out of Israel where they were having all their pains and trouble and trials and everything, though they complained all the way. I told the children the other day. I said, "Now, one thing you got to learn to stop doing is complaining because that's part of it. The Israelites . . . I mean the Egyptians, the Israelites come out of Egypt and complained every step of the way: Now, if we had stayed back yonder in Egypt. If we had stayed back there."

And, in fact, they were hollering, "Lord help me." And that's the way we are today.

Traditionally, Moses represented an important biblical figure in the African American folk cultural tradition. In 1865, a newcomer to the South noted that to enslaved Africans, "Moses is their ideal of all that is high and noble and perfect, in man." As in these narrative samples, the miracles that Moses performed endear him as a folk hero. He has the powers of the conjurer and the wisdom of a teacher.

For many informants, the interview developed into a social visit, and personal experience narratives became the primary vehicle for disclosure. Wiregrass inhabitants share their life histories with each other, thereby increasing the prevalence of certain motifs. Wiregrass, itself a motif, figures conspicuously in the narratives of many older adults as an undomesticated resource containing certain hidden dangers. In its unburnt state, wiregrass was an integral part of the terrain and served as cover for wildlife. Milton Young, an African American in Wiregrass Florida, reported:

> I liked to got rattlesnake bit one day. I was squirrel hunting on this track of land. I was hunting squirrels and a bunch of quails flew up and lit out. I said "Well, I'm going to get me some of them." I went out there and tried to get me some quail. They were out there in grass, you know. I didn't rush on him. I just kept backing up and backing up. And I just happened to look down, and I was close to one [a snake] from here to your handbag. He was already coiled up.

As a result, Young said, he had given up hunting. Fred Smith, an African American undertaker, reported a similar account of a snake as more of an occupational hazard:

> Mostly, you know, I generally walked behind—in front—of the fellow that be carrying the casket to the grave. We had to go a certain distance. So, on my way in front of him, I saw a rattlesnake. It looked like he was that large. Come right across. In that wiregrass, you couldn't see nothing. I was scared to tell the people who had the casket behind me. See, I just slowed up until he crawled, and they were coming along slowly with the casket. So when we got there, I went back, and I got in the car. That thing scared me. I was scared to go back to the car because I didn't know which way he decided to go. You know? We have some devil of things in the funeral business.

Snakes are another frequent motif in the everyday narrative accounts of Wiregrass residents. Connie Palmer, a Wiregrass Florida resident of Creek Indian descent, met a snake at her front door:

> I called my husband over the telephone; and over the telephone, he was telling me what to do [how to load a shotgun]. And so I got it loaded. I failed to tell

him that it was on the porch. I stood in the door and shot seven times and there's a brick wall behind where the snake was laying. It's a wonder that I didn't ricochet and kill myself. I shot the heck out of the lawn chair. I killed him. When he came home and saw where I had shot, he had a fit and said: "Don't you ever shoot at a brick wall again." I said, "Could you tell by my voice that I was a little agitated and upset and completely stupid?" It was a horrible experience.

Snakes often figure in cautionary tales. As E. W. Carswell, a native of Wiregrass Florida, observed, "Maybe we've instinctively feared snakes, since our distant ancestors feared and distrusted them for centuries. Remember the role the serpent played in the Garden of Eden? They were once worshipped as gods or friends of the gods, and they have been symbols of wealth, knowledge or wisdom in some parts of the ancient world. In ancient Greece, they were associated with the God of Medicine."

Because snakes were both feared and highly prevalent, a class of individuals arose who could dispose of them. Bessie Jones, one of the famed Sea Island Singers, lived in and on the fringes of Wiregrass for most of her life. She speaks of a snake catcher in her memoirs: "He had some kind of funny stuff on him but he was a snake charmer. He blew that thing in his mouth and the snakes came right around him as though he had called chickens that were his pets. They came up and wrapped themselves around him, all around his neck, and he would just grab one, jerk its mouth open and put his hand in there and pull out that bag. . . . He got about 48 out of the woods."

In 1977, folklorist Dave Stanley interviewed Roy Dominy. Dominy spoke of Uncle Guy Fuller, a more contemporary snake catcher. In passing, Dominy (as paraphrased by Stanley) offered an explanation for the ubiquitous rattlers. "They're becoming more prevalent. On his farm, rattlesnakes were pretty well extinguished years ago—none killed for 40 years. Now, they're coming back, perhaps because they're chased out of timber during logging operations. Also woods no longer burned."

Other motifs in Wiregrass narratives involve religious conversions and "conjure tales." The buried treasure motif in a personal experience narrative probably generates the most curiosity. African American storyteller Milton Young provided the following context for his narrative: "People in slavery time didn't have no banks and they would kill somebody and bury it with that money they tell me. They were thinking that they were protecting the money. The spirit would appear and make you leave it." Young recalled the following personal attempt to recover buried treasure:

Seven-five-three-or-nine—to dig money you have to have a hard number. My grandmother got her three boys and got four more men. They were all related you know, and they even had me down there. I made seven now, and a man from Birmingham really had a machine. And it went to singing when he got to a certain place. "Gentlemen, let me tell you this machine will find oil just as well as money. And if its an oil well, you know what that means?" An oil well—"If an oil well, will you be willing for every man to have a share?" He said, "No—that gets it then. We won't dig." You have to deal fair or it won't work. That man went on back. He gathered up his tools and went on back, and we figured that we'd get it. We men said since we done found the spot, all right we'll go on down there. And we got to digging. They say don't talk while you digging. Don't say nothing to nobody. We got down about waist deep. Whenever one man would get tired, he wouldn't say, "You dig some" or "I'm tired you dig some." You weren't supposed to say that. We got down there waist deep. He laid down the shovel and hollered, "Doc Thomas, get off my back! Doc Thomas get off my back!" This was in the day time; it wasn't at night. Everybody said, "You ready to go?" So, we ain't been back there no more.

As this tale indicates, an assortment of folk beliefs accompanied the practice of treasure hunting. Success depended upon a system of inviolate rules governing diverse numerological and related concrete symbols. The tale also incorporates elements that help locate the event not in the remote past but in the near present, such as technology and oil, a newfound source of wealth. The incorporation of technologically sophisticated equipment with a spirit guard is also consistent with this tale type.

The gothic South emerges through its folk narrative and literary traditions. The persistence of supernatural tales is sometimes cited as evidence that the South is the world's most bedeviled region. In the context of Wiregrass Country, the memorates express not merely helplessness in the face of the mysterious supernatural but courage. They eloquently show their narrators' application to reality of a system of religious belief according to which all things work together for the general good. These narrators have a hearty respect for the supernatural world and also the scriptural "faith as a grain of mustard seed." Within the spiritual arena of residents of Wiregrass Country, all things are possible.

PART THREE

Recreation and Leisure

CHAPTER 7

Games, Gatherings, and Special Occasions

Wiregrass families historically worked hard and played hard. Story teller Allie Ben Prince said that his secret for continued good health was "hard work and frolicking." The nature of the hard work, and the time available for leisure, in the Wiregrass as in most agrarian societies depended on the season. When there was too much work to do, farmers satisfied the need for recreation by making work into play. Play, of course, is not only relief from work but also a form of artistic communication. People when they play are simultaneously interpreting their lives socially, politically, and economically.

During the year, Wiregrass farmers and their families traditionally engaged in several get-togethers termed husking bees or corn shuckings, cane grindings or sugar boilings, "pindar" (peanut) shellings and boilings, and hog killings. Several activities revolved around the growth of peanuts. "Pindar shellings are quite popular now with the young people. They meet at the place appointed and after shelling pindars for a while, work is laid aside and the remainder of the evening is spent in social games, music, and conversation. It is always work before play." For best results, peanuts had to be shelled, since the pods were needed to produce the next crop. J. L. Herring, a local writer, described the process: "After the Christmas holidays, in the midst of the spring plowing, we went over to Jim's to shell his peanuts for him—only we did not call them peanuts then—the new name has come with modern machinery and the commercializing of the peanut. It was as good, old-fashioned groundpeas that we knew them. And all farmers were not finicky about having their groundpeas shelled for planting—they just dropped 'em in, hull and all, and trusted to luck." After they completed the shelling, they raced and played games. For refreshments, some of the peanuts were covered with syrup to make "groundpea candy," considered a real treat. Afterward, "chairs were set back against the wall. The bed had been taken down already. One of the boys had a harmonica and two had jew's harps. This trio were given seats of honor, in the chimney corner, partners were chosen, the music started up, and to it were added fresh young voices in song."

In contrast, peanut boiling occurred during the summer months, when there was a lull in the work schedule. This form of work was not labor intensive, as E. W. Carswell recalled it. "The boiled peanuts were delicacies indeed, but equally important perhaps, they contributed to the social climate of our community. Without them, we would have had to find some other reason for staging a party." Life itself, and not just a livelihood, depended on the food crops that created the occasion for celebration. Corn shuckings, hog killings, and peanut shellings brought families welcome reinforcements from the community labor pool, and the opportunity for fun and games ensured that the work got done to the benefit of all.

At first, fearful of American Indians, settlers depended on one another for security. Later they grew to be interdependent in many other ways. Cane grindings, log rolling and splitting, and barn raisings were difficult, labor-intensive jobs—arduous work that could be unpleasant, if not downright impossible, to do alone. Tasks of monumental proportion became more manageable when they were tackled collectively with community zeal. In this way Wiregrass folks' communal spirit helped secure the necessities of life.

Quilting parties and sewing bees offered women opportunities for the same communal and social interaction—with the same benefits—as the heavier tasks did the men. The two often occurred together, as the following account, provided by Herring, illustrates.

> John, the son of Farmer Jim, was soon to wed Sally, the daughter of Farmer Joe, and this houseraising was part of his home-building. . . . Two older men experienced in such work took charge of the young men, divided in squads. . . . Mrs. Jim had pieced two quilt-tops during the winter evenings, and to quilt these while the house was being raised the women-folks had been invited. . . . After dinner there was a short period of recreation—flirting, quoit-pitching, mayhap wrestling or jumping, as inclination led, and then back to work. Before night, John's house was "raised."

Because houses lacked central heating, you needed a quilt if you wanted to be warm at night in bed. The manufacture of quilts for everyday use was therefore an important local activity. Neighborhood women regularly assembled for quilting bees, which sometimes occurred while another event, such as cane grinding, was occupying the men. Wires with hooks were hung from the ceiling so that two poles could conveniently be attached to the quilting frame in order to make better use of available space. According to historian Fred Watson, the women led a mundane existence unless they were doing something together: "When a farmer had work to do which required outside labor he would ask his neighbors for help. Life was more monotonous for the women than the men for they had more work to do, and were tied more closely at home. If they had neighbors close enough, visits were exchanged, and they would converse while they sewed, knitted or quilted."

Ophelia White, an African American quilter, told how the women consciously passed their art on to another generation:

They also went from house to house doing that. They would take us with them. They would say we are going over to . . . My Husband's great aunt named me. They would say we are going over to Sarah Marshall's house and quilt today. All the women had their own quilting frame so it wasn't like you had to bring yours along. They would start off cutting us out little tiny scraps but they were straight scraps . . . , quilt scraps. And they would give you a needle and a thread and you could sit there if you got where you wanted to come in and got interested. And you could put your little pieces together also. And if enough children were interested enough, and they would get it big enough . . . Just like we would do so many, and then the children at other houses, that mothers and grandmothers were involved in this quilting thing, then they would get it together and the parents would put . . . take my pieces and put them with Sarah Marshall's grandchildren's pieces and the other lady's grandchild pieces until they get enough to get a quilt together. And they would all sew them all together for us. And until everybody that was involved in it . . . each family had a quilt coming from those children. If it didn't look good, that was yours. Then, they would lay it out on the floor, and they would put what they call padding. Then, they would put the lining on the back, and they would just tack the lining together enough so they could put our little quilt frame thing down. And they would help us to get started. And a lot of times, they didn't look very good until you grew into doing it. Then, as I grew older, I loved to quilt and still love to quilt.

Entertainment centered around the farm, the river, the town, the church, and the school. When the work had been finished, people would play. They often danced to fiddle tunes all night or until the liquor ran out. And some times people got carried away.

One man had a rail splittin' at his place where about 750 rails were split. His wife had baked up lots of pies to eat, but Bill Osborne slipped in an' stole his arms full of these 'tater pies. Then they started dancin' an' got into a fight. Old man Bill Page run an' knocked th' gate down; Will Campbell tore th' partition out of the house to have more room fur dancin'. One man got a kid under each arm an' run fur th' boat, but he missed the wharf an' was out in th' Bay shoulder deep callin' fur somebody to bring a boat.

Disruptive behavior took other forms as well on such special occasions. "Sometimes the wife of the pioneer would get 'mad' and take her rocking chair and set it in the middle of the dance floor. There she would sit, rocking. The dancers would carry her out, chair and all, but she would come right back. If they were able to 'soothe her feelings,' she would permit them to continue the dance. If not, the dance would be broken up for that night." Accounts such as these vividly recreate the social texture of a bygone era.

Of all the reasons why people gathered together, cutting a bee tree is perhaps the most intriguing to the modern reader. First, someone with patience and a keen eye tracked a bee to its hive. By invitation, neighbors assembled on a Saturday night, when the bees would be more listless. Herring described the procedure:

> The folks came at early candle light, a fire was built, and the axe-men went to work. One on either side, they soon had the tree almost ready to fall. . . . The men hurried up just as the bees, recovering from the shock of fall, angry and buzzing, came out. Rags were fired, and with the smudge from the pine-boughs the bees were driven back or out of the way of the workers. . . . The honey lay in long, golden layers of soft comb up and down the hollow. . . . After the honey was gathered, the bees were left to buzz around the ruins of their home and arrange to start another, while all went to Uncle George's house near by. The women folks had gone ahead and before we arrived the waffle irons were hot.

The honey fresh from the comb was then served on hot waffles.

For respite from their workaday lives, Wiregrass families often took excursions to the Gulf of Mexico. Once they arrived, they gathered saltwater fish to vary their diets. According to scholar Elsie Surber: "At one time 'up the country' people came to the bay in covered wagons to get salt fish and oysters to take back home with them. While they were here, they would make an outing of it. They camped out and friends from this section would gather in and there would be singing, storytelling, and a general good time. In later years, people went on weekend camping trips on the creeks for recreation. They would take tents and bedding for sleeping out and equipment for catching and cooking fish."

Wiregrass families relish fishing, and they also like seafood, which they cannot readily obtain. Oysters and mullet, being hard to get, are considered great delicacies. These are saltwater species, which must be imported from the Gulf. Consumption of these foods has traditionally been restricted to certain months of the year. According to Carswell, "The finest, most fla-

vorful oysters in the world thus became abundantly available to hinterland-
ers—sometimes as far north as Eufaula, Alabama, and Columbus, Georgia—at bargain basement prices. Eating raw oysters from the half-shell
soon became a common custom. In fact it was almost an addiction during
the 'R' months, from September to April."

A century ago, oysters were as popular as hotdogs are today. Oyster suppers were common during the early 1900s and became the pillar of fund-
raising activities, especially during election years. Travelers to the Gulf
Coast could not bring back enough oysters to satisfy their friends.

Mullet is as popular as oysters in the Wiregrass region and is subject to
the same seasonal restrictions. Although it can now readily be purchased
in markets year round, many residents still do not eat this fish during the
summer months. Folklorist Dave Stanley interviewed Bobby Roberts and
recorded that "Mullet season is cotton-picking time; after they got in the
first bale of cotton, Robert's father would go to town and bring back a mess
of mullet and a dozen lemons—the traditional combination is mullet and
lemonade, both being relatively expensive and rare, the latter because of
the shortage of fresh fruit and the rarity of ice."

Before the availability of refrigeration, traditionally, fish from the coast
had to be salt cured in order to preserve it. Carswell observed: "Few people
today seem to like salt-cured mullet. Some haven't even heard of the delicacy, and many who have might insist that the word delicacy is grossly
misused in describing salt-cured fish of any kind. It is all a matter of taste,
I suppose, and I just happen to like the taste of salt-cured mullet. Especially
for breakfast."

Although the mode of transportation varied over the decades, the trek to
the Gulf for a vacation of sorts clearly became a tradition. Carswell described the effect of the invention of the automobile on these visits: "Going
from the heart of the Wiregrass Country to the Gulf on a Model T Ford
was an exciting adventure back in the early 1930s. And it required patience
and stamina too. The 90-mile drive required from 10–12 hours, depending
on how many times we had to stop and change tires, refill the radiator or
push through a boggy place, a sand bed or up some hill." In Wiregrass
Alabama, people without cars took excursion trains on the Bay Line, which
departed every Sunday to Panama City.

As towns developed within Wiregrass Country, parties became more the-
matic and orderly. There were birthday parties, ice cream socials, social
dances, candy pullings, and "tacky" (or "tackie") parties. A tacky party
required participants to dress up as caricatures of a past stereotype of themselves. The *Cairo Messenger* reported: "The judges proclaimed Miss Fleta
Powell and Mr. Charles Beale the most original crackers present to whom
were awarded prizes." Such parties gave participants the chance to poke

fun at the past and, through play, to distance themselves from the cracker image imposed on their ancestors.

The increase in number and refinement of these leisure events in the towns also reflected a change in the everyday lives of the people. Town living was less physically demanding than life in the country. Consequently, residents could devote their leisure to more relaxed, and more relaxing, pursuits.

In Wiregrass Country dancing was not predictably popular, since many fundamentalist churches considered it to be sinful. According to Ted Ownby, evangelicals found themselves in a difficult position whenever there was a social gathering: "Some even spoke as though dancing could break out unexpectedly against their wishes; the price of dance-free homes was eternal vigilance."

Arthur Powell, a local writer, spoke of the ingenious ways that people found to circumvent religious restrictions. "Frequently, we would have parties at the various homes of the town. We were not allowed to dance— that was against the rules of the church—but we played 'Tucker' and 'twistification.' The former was simply the old fashioned square dance under another name, and the latter a somewhat modified version of the Virginia Reel." Herring has provided words to "Twistification" and described its movements:

> Oh, come along, my pretty miss;
> Oh, come along, my honey!
> Oh, come along, my sweet sugar-lump
> And we won't go home 'till Monday.
> And now I turn my sugar and tea;
> And now I turn my honey;
> And now I turn my sugar and tea
> And now I turn my darling.

The dance itself, he said, "partook very much of the form of the old Virginia reel, the first four lines being sung to a quick march by the leading couple between the lines of the others, and the last four lines as they swung opposites and each other, the 'sugar and tea' being opposite and the 'honey' and 'darling' the partner." Clearly people found ways of having fun without running afoul of the church.

By 1911, social customs began to change in areas like Statesboro, Georgia, as outsiders arrived with different religious backgrounds and cultural expectations. The change elicited comments in editorials like the following: "If there was a law on the statute books against men and women taking charge of a public hotel in which the church people hold a majority of the stock and making merry until late hours of the night for the edification of the traveling men who have turned in for a night's rest they would stop, but there is no such law and hence it goes on; goes on for the reason that a majority of the town wants it to go on, and the best people turn out and participate in it."

Dancing was a volatile issue for churchgoers, of course, because of its sexual overtones. The fundamentalists associated dancing with sexual promiscuity. Any time young people assembled, whether at church or in the homes, courtship was thought to be the objective. More recently Connie Palmer, a resident of Altha, Florida, recalled a popular form of childhood courtship. In this "yard play," neighborhood children joined in games like Flying Dutchman, Drop the Handkerchief, and Drugstore. To play Drugstore, each child took the name of a candy product and would say, for instance, "I want Baby Ruth." Children would then pair off as a couple, link arms, and walk down the road to a designated spot and back. They played without adult supervision, and they considered the game a "safe way to court."

Play commonly affords opportunities for conforming to social norms and for departing from them. Serving as exercises of power, games routinely offer youngsters the chance to subvert the existing system. Pranks are one traditional way of doing so. Folklorist Mariella Hartsfield has described "the dumb-bull," a simple folk object fashioned like a drum with a cord laced through it. When the cord was pulled, the contraption produced a hideous noise and thereby conferred some social control on the noise-maker. Hartsfield reported:

> Different stories abound in the local area about one item of material culture—the dumb-bull—which was still in existence in the early part of this century. It was notorious primarily as a prankster's tool or toy, it could be used to achieve more serious results, such as ridding a neighborhood of undesirables. The dumb-bull was a device that emitted a harrowing, hair-raising roar reminiscent of a wild bull, a lion, a panther, or some ungodly monster. The roar was so effective that it could be heard two or three miles on a quiet night and could cause livestock to break out of stalls and stampede.

According to Hartsfield, the dumb-bull served three functions: it could be a prank played on friends, foes, and rivals; a means of frightening African Americans, whom the whites deemed indolent, shiftless, and superstitious; and a trick aimed at discouraging people generally considered undesirable.

Many pranks by their nature seem to have helped youngsters vent their frustrations. Their families, schools, and churches characteristically demanded strict obedience. The following incident, described by a local historian in Wiregrass Georgia, indicates that young pranksters had no qualms about making unsuspecting women their victims:

A lady spent the week-end with some good friends of hers. The boys of the family were up to no good! She may have taken their bed and they had to sleep on a pallet on the floor or perhaps they did not think too much of her. At any rate, one young fellow swiped her black stockings; these were in vogue in the twenties or thirties. The boys then carefully turned them wrong side out, rubbed them up and down the back of the chimney as if cleaning it, turned them right side out, and returned them to the visitor's room. When time came to dress, not realizing anything was amiss, the lady put on her stockings and proceeded to the meeting place for the foot-washing. Imagine her discomfort and chagrin, when she removed her stockings!

Institutions of local government were also the butt of childish pranks. One county historian reported that "at one time it was the favorite sport of rowdy boys to drive the goats in the wide court house double doors at night, up the stairs, and out the windows of the court room."

Wiregrass adults today enjoy recalling pranks that they themselves played. Bertha Wrice, an African American, recalled torturing chickens by pinning their wings back so that they tipped over. Owen Wrice, Bertha's husband, said that he and his brothers used to bronco ride the family bull. "We'd catch the old bull and ride him all across the field."

Solitary children found completely different forms of recreation. The early toys of Wiregrass children tended to be self-constructed, homemade items. For boys, toy weapons that required shooting skill prevailed. According to William Rogers, the historian, "In the 1870s young boys in Thomasville became shots with what were called 'Alabama slings' (in time their accuracy drew warnings that slingshots should not be employed against street lamps, windowpanes, stock, or fowls)." By the 1880s boys' fancy had turned to popguns constructed out of hollowed-out elderberry wood with a strong stick as a plunger and green chinaberry as ammunition. Children could put anything in the environment to use. Carswell credits himself with having revolutionized play for a while by making a bow with arrows: "Within days, nearly everybody in the neighborhood had built himself a bow and some arrows. No one, until the bow and arrow craze ran its brief course, was willing to be seen with a slingshot."

Dorothy Brannen, a local historian in Bulloch County, Georgia, said that in 1912, boys created their own pushmobiles and raced them around the courthouse square. In time, these races gained community sanction, and nearly 1,000 people assembled to watch the events. The winners received a dollar prize. Brannen quotes contemporary news reports: "An event of interest was the pushmobile race about the court house square last Friday afternoon, in which seven machines participated. Besides the driver, there were four pushers to each machine, making a total of thirty-five boys engaged." The boys completed ten laps, or an approximate distance of one and a half miles.

Other homemade items showed great resourcefulness and precision. Ophelia White recalled:

> We didn't have television until we was . . . I guess that I was maybe twelve when we got a television. But we didn't seem to be lonesome or anything for entertainment. Because at night, we would get out there and my brothers would make what we would call a packer. You would take a syrup can and it had a little tiny lid on it at the time. And we would put dirt in it. . . . some dirt and some rocks and run a wire through it all the way through it so that it would roll good. That was a lot of fun because you would race one another with it. And then we had this thing called a tin walker. You could take a tin can and run a wire through. . . . okay, where you open it that part would go on the ground. And you would run a wire through the top part of it and you could hold it up and you could walk on it. You would have two of those cans. And that was a lot of fun. Everybody had their own private tin walker and everyone would have their own private packer. So you knew not to get so and so's.

Children created objects to amuse themselves and so that they could compete against each other. Many adults reminisce about the hours of joy provided by found objects such as car tires or car rims. Even games like checkers took on a communal flare. Children commonly played a version of "rise and fly," with the winner taking on challengers both young and old. They played together in semipublic spaces in the yard or beside the tobacco barn.

Play, as a kind of communication, had other functions in Wiregrass Country. Ball games have long had a significant role in human existence. American Indians within the Wiregrass played chunkee, a ball game having ritual and ceremonial importance. Fireball was another type of American Indian ball game though one known mostly from local oral history. One of the few written references to it comes from observation of a game of fireball being played on the Tuscarora Indian Reservation near Niagara Falls, New York, in July 1986. Local elders on the reservation described the game as a traditional pastime throughout the Iroquois confederacy.

> This game is appropriately named because the playing implement is a ball of fire, that is, burning material that takes approximately twenty minutes to be completely consumed. Although it is roughly the same as soccer, fireball is a nighttime game played in total darkness except for small torches to mark the perimeters of the goals, and the ball itself is burning.
>
> Prior to the game the ball was prepared by wrapping it in an extensive amount of cloth, tying it with cords, and binding it with soft, wire mesh to

hold it together. After all this wrapping, the ball, which was approximately the size of a soccer ball, was placed in flammable fluid until thoroughly soaked.

After the goal markers had been lighted, the players were taken to the center of the field where the ball was set aflame, and the game commenced. The fiery ball was advanced by kicking, in the same manner as in soccer, and players were permitted to bat the ball or throw it without penalty. However, the burning ball itself tended to discourage extensive use of this privilege. Most players wore shoes during the game, and the goalkeepers were allowed to wear gloves. Each time the ball was kicked it would blaze even brighter with the stimulation of additional oxygen to the burning material. The game lasted approximately twenty minutes before the ball was totally consumed, and the team leading at that time was declared the winner. Though less serious than some other ball games, fireball appeared to be a favorite for both players and spectators.

The game of fireball was widespread among the American Indians, and they introduced it to inhabitants within Wiregrass Country.

Fireball is like wiregrass itself in not being known to everyone within the historic region. There are nevertheless several detailed descriptions of the sport from Sylvester, Georgia, to Altha, Florida. Boysie McGriff, an African American, described a version of fireball that he played as a child in Cairo, Georgia:

Say, about sundown, then all the neighbors be already planned that before time. And sometime it would be like a hundred of them would come. And they take a washtub and put kerosene in it over here. And, on the other side of the field, they'd have another washtub over here with kerosene in it. And then you build a fire over here. And then all of us would get together—this bunch on this side of the field, and we be on this side of the field. And then we would war with one another with our fireball. Sometimes we hit one another with the fireball like that, and we kept on until one side won.

The ball consisted of a burlap sack tied together with a fine rope. When it hit you, it would harmlessly bounce off.

Adults sometimes played the game together with their children. Ophelia White recalled a game played in celebration of her mother's birthday in Sylvester, Georgia:

Fireballing that was like your birthday party. That was a party. They would roast peanuts and . . . uh that was more or less their type of entertainment. They would take old rags and soak them in kerosene. And they would roll them up real tight and they had haywire at the time that you can't find that anymore. And those men would roll that haywire around those rags that had been soaked in that kerosene. And they would make a ball about that big then put a piece of haywire on it that long so that it could stay away from your hand. And if the party was going to be tomorrow (and normally it would be on Saturday night) if the party was going to be tomorrow night, then they had already soaked them during that week in kerosene. Then after they rolled them, they would set them back over in a bucket of kerosene again to make sure that they were still saturated with it. Then they would light it. They would have a fire out in the yard, well out in the field because it would always come like after your peanuts and things have been out of ground and all this stuff. Then you have an open ground field out there because in January there's nothing growing out there that could be set a fire. And they would go out and right on the edge of that field was where they would set the fire. And you would light that fireball and you would run around across the field and you would just whirl it around and you would throw it just as far as you could. It was as if you were throwing at another person because they have theirs too. And it was a lot of fun. Even when we were small, they would make little ones for the children. Because they would bring, other people who would come to party would bring their children. That was the entertainment for the children and the adults.

Connie Palmer, who claims Creek ancestry, described the sport as "something frisky for young folk." McGriff said: "When you see that fireball in the night, when it was black dark like that, that was beautiful."

Townball was a game of European origin, a forerunner of modern baseball, ritualized by formal institutions like schools. Town ball preceded baseball and differed from it in many ways. Balls, like most toys, were laboriously constructed by hand. According to Brannen,

> The ball used was home-made, the work of many patient hours. First, for the thread, a pair of home knit socks, worn beyond hope of repair, was necessary. These were cut off at the ankle and the cut ends picked out until the unbroken thread was reached. Then, hour after hour, the threads of the sock were raveled and wound into the ball. . . . The batter used a paddle with a wide blade, usually made from a board which had seen better days, with one end trimmed with a pocket-knife until it could be grasped with the hand. . . . There were no umpires and no professional pitchers. Anybody pitched, and nearly everybody caught.

Balls were often lost in the wiregrass on the fields unless the foliage had been destroyed by the plow.

Baseball has its own tradition in Wiregrass Country and was as central to life there as singing conventions and the caning of sugar. After the D & S Railroad had been built, Dover, Georgia, for example, became a favorite spot for picnics and ball games. A printed notice of a big picnic to be held at Dover in 1894 reads: "The colored people of Statesboro will have an excursion to Dover on Saturday the 11th inst., at the low rate of 30 cents for adults and 20 cents for children. A match game of ball will be played by picked nines, and R. E. Wright and W. E. Moore and perhaps other prominent colored speakers, will address the crowd. Everybody is invited. Don't forget the day." For African Americans, baseball games also were linked to Emancipation Day celebrations.

In the Wiregrass of the 1890s, baseball enthusiasts played the game viciously and with vengeance. Fred Watson has indicated that "pistols, billies and other equipment [were] necessary to play baseball in that era." The sport was not yet locally idealized as a means of socializing the economically and culturally deprived.

Like sports, holidays had a flavor quite their own within Wiregrass Country. Thanksgiving Day, with its origins in New England, did not become a holiday of note until about 1890. Thereafter it became associated with the region's hunting traditions. According to Dorothy Brannen, in Bulloch County, Georgia, "Some went hunting, some went riding, some went to church, and some staid at home. Most of them went gunning, either for birds or bigger game. One crowd went down on the S & S to Ivanhoe, where a drive for deer had been planned. They also carried pointers, and indicated they might shoot a quail if one attacked them." The day had religious significance for many churchgoers, who attended holiday observances and regarded the occasion as one meant for devotion rather than sport. Still other residents celebrated the day as a "Harvest Home Festival" and gave thanks for their harvest.

There was also an annual Thanksgiving turkey shoot. As Ted Ownby has written, "The traditional Southern belief in the necessity of being armed, combined with the hunter's joy in skillful marksmanship and the general male zest for competition, made shooting contests enormously popular." The competition at first involved live turkeys that had been tethered. Contestants, who paid a nominal fee, shot rounds of ammunition from a prescribed distance. To win a bird, the contestant needed to show good marksmanship by shooting a bird in the head. In later years, inanimate targets were substituted, and turkeys were reserved as the prize.

For a long time, Christmas was observed in no distinctive fashion peculiar to the region. Children received as gifts only fruit and a few nuts, and there was no tradition of decorating a Christmas tree. One African American remembered the family celebration: "During Christmas season, Mama and Papa would go to town and get some apples and oranges for us. Then on Christmas Day, we would each have a shoe box with an apple, an orange, some raisins, and if mama had enough money, some nuts, inside. And she'd always make each of us a little something, like a rag doll." By and large, families celebrated Christmas in their own different ways.

The Christmas season offered a great time for visiting and parties. In Wiregrass Florida, Surber has noted "serenading," which resembled caroling and may have been a form of Christmas mumming. Ownby states that males "learned early to be loud and competitive during the holiday season, drawing attention to their presence by firing guns and more often, by setting off fireworks." The *Bulloch Times* in 1896 reported: "The pop of the firecracker, the whir and bang of the skyrocket and the bleating of the tin horn for the past few evenings would impress one that Christmas had come." Firecrackers were reserved for celebrating Christmas rather than July 4. According to another source, "People too poor to afford firecrackers for Christmas celebrations substituted forest fires." Christmas trees in the home are a relatively recent innovation.

Some residents conspicuously celebrated "Old Christmas." Carswell said, "They never explained, at least to my satisfaction, the background of the 'Old Christmas' tradition. I remember references, however, to the '14 days of Christmas,' which I believe consisted of the last eight days of Dec. and the first 6 day of January. It was the last of those days, January 6, that was once observed as 'Old Christmas.'" Several legends and beliefs were also connected with this period. It was said, for example, that in the early hours of Old Christmas morning, the barnyard animals kneeled and prayed aloud in celebration of Christ's birth. Carswell also reports the belief that the weather conditions on the twelve days preceding Old Christmas foretold the weather for the year ahead.

New Year's day was also observed as an extension of the Christmas season. Many African American churches still hold Watch Night services—gatherings to watch the old year go out and the new year come in—on New Year's Eve and consider it a time for spiritual reflection on the coming year.

African Americans traditionally commemorated their freedom on New Year's Day by reading the Emancipation Proclamation at solemn public gatherings. According to William Rogers, "A typical ceremony was held in 1892 when hundreds of blacks gathered to pray, to hear the document intoned, to listen to other speeches, and to enjoy a meal."

On New Year's Day people ate a traditional dinner of pork, blackeyed peas, and greens as elsewhere throughout the South. One local Wiregrass resident explained that there were "peas for peace, jowls for joy, and collards for dollars." Surber claimed that the meal "was supposed to bring prosperity during the coming year to those who ate it."

Until about 1875, Independence Day had held little significance in the Wiregrass. After the Civil War, however, southern veterans made it into a celebration of the "Lost Cause." Herring recalled that "there was not much of a display of Old Glory, for too many men were alive to whom the flag brought unpleasant memories; but the speech was pretty much the same; the barbecue almost the same." And he said that the day gradually improved as the hours passed: "After dinner, the speaker gone, the platform gave place to the fiddlers, the strawbeaters, the caller and the dancing couples. . . . the young folks still stepping lively to the jingling tune of the 'Arkansas Traveler,' or one of his many kindred, or

> Johnny, get your hair cut, hair cut, hair cut
> Johnny, get your hair cut, shave and shine,
> Johnny, get your hair cut, hair cut, hair cut
> Johnny, get your hair cut, just like mine.

Ultimately, the holiday evolved into a full-fledged celebration with most of its present-day features: picnics, barbecues, bands, and contests.

By the turn of the century, picnics dominated the milder seasons in Wiregrass Country. Sunday school picnics filled the local residents' annual calendar of events. People also organized family picnics and big public ones, usually at one of the plentiful rivers. Several commercial sites built permanent picnic facilities to satisfy the local crowd. These included elevated pavilions for dancing and, according to local historian Georgia Griffin, "a pool hall, a self-playing piano, and a commissary offering assorted groceries." Advertisements in the local press at the turn of the century suggest that the well-planned picnic required such sundry items as seeded raisins, currants, prunes, dates, and shredded coconuts. Cakes, rare treats, were made in quantity almost exclusively for festive occasions. In addition, picnics featured contests of all kinds. On the Gulf, rowboat races attracted competitors. The climbing of a greasy pole fascinated both onlookers and participants and highlighted many local festivities until recent years.

Emancipation Day still holds special memories for many African Americans today and was a more spirited occasion than New Year's Day. Many people cannot recall exactly when it ceased being celebrated as a holiday. Many middle-aged people remember participating in celebrations well into the 1950s. Some believe that it declined in popularity when African Americans entered the wage labor force in greater numbers. In the past, revelers traditionally celebrated Emancipation Day on the actual day that their forebears received news of the Proclamation. This date varied throughout the Wiregrass region and throughout the South. In Wiregrass Georgia, federal troops did not arrive with the message until May 20, 1865, and in Wiregrass Alabama and Florida, May 28 was the date, but in faraway Texas (where the event is still actively observed), federal troops did not bring word until Juneteenth (June 19, 1865). According to tradition, even if the date fell on a weekday, everyone took the day off to celebrate. Emancipation Day celebrations are being revived today as an expression of pride and community solidarity, but few celebrations occur on the exact date, as in the past.

Many African Americans regarded Independence Day as separate from their own holiday. William Rogers provided the following account:

> In 1895 blacks at Metcalfe held a mammoth Emancipation Day that was attended by people from the surrounding area. Both whites and blacks in the 1880s and 1890s liked to get groups together and take train "excursions" to nearby towns. Fire companies, Sunday school classes, and other organizations would coordinate plans with kindred orders in neighboring towns, secure reduced railroad rates and then begin the excursion. The train ride to and from the destination was as enjoyable as the event itself. If anything blacks held more excursions than whites, and May 20 seemed to be a natural day to celebrate. In 1899, Emancipation Day saw blacks from Valdosta, Bainbridge, and Thomasville converge on Albany for a massive celebration.

This celebration amounted to a feast day and offered a far greater range of food than any other holiday in the year. Any mention of Emancipation Day usually elicits a fully enumerated list of menu items. McGriff recalled "five barrels of lemonade, and the cakes, all the churches bring food and stuff. Just like you were going to a funeral or something. And sometimes they had tables slammed to the end of the row here. And they had ice cream and cake." Boards were stretched across wire fencing to make tables for the diners.

Chicken pilaf, often mentioned as a festive food, is still being made by social organizations to raise funds. Owen Wrice of Lanier County remembered the dish: "One of the most enjoyable things I think we had at the picnic was that chicken and rice cooked in the washpot. They would clean that washpot and they cook that chicken and rice in that washpot and I'll tell you that was something tasty." The same dish was sometimes made with turkey for Emancipation Day: "Do you know how to make purlow? Take three or four turkeys and put it in your pot and boil it until it comes to pieces. Then throw the bones out of it and put so many pounds of rice in there and stir it up and put purlow, barbecue, rice and all that stuff in there."

Mother's Day is doubly significant for residents of the Wiregrass, being remembered in part as Decoration Day. In her history of Bay County, Florida, Elsie Surber associated it with a "patriotic program held in the cemetery and flowers were put on all the graves." A strictly southern observance, the day allowed Confederate women to show solidarity with their men.

African Americans, who by custom revere the deceased, adopted the holiday as a time for decorating the graveside. Bessie Jones, a longtime resident of Wiregrass Georgia, described the practice:

> People decorated the graves back then if they wanted to. Sometimes the dead person had a habit of certain things they liked to eat out of or certain things they liked to drink out of or a picture they liked—they put them on the graves. I don't know what they put them there for—to entertain, I guess. I don't know. And they'd punch holes in the bottom of the glasses and such—maybe to keep out snakes and other things from settling there. I put flowers on my mother's grave. But when you do a thing like that, be sure you put a hole in what ever you have the flowers in.

In the South, people have many ways of honoring their dead.

Folklorists and other scholars have found African antecedents for many burial customs. John Vlach, who has widely researched graveyard decorations, remarked that "Black Graves are made distinct by the placement of a wide variety of offerings on the top of the burial mound." His observation is borne out by a survey of the graveyards of small rural churches in Wiregrass Country.

African American funerary customs demand an extended period of mourning that may have scriptural origins. Boysie McGriff mentioned "seven days of silence with the dead. They put you on a cooling board and come and have prayer and all that. I think that they did that because they probably thought about the time when Job was sick and they mourned Job about seven days."

Funerary customs, too, incorporate customs found in Africa and throughout the African diaspora. Tommie Gabriel of Thomas County, Georgia, recalled:

> Here's an illustration of something when I was a boy. And we had somebody die on the . . . we'd call it the plantation out there. (It isn't exactly a plantation as you know but its more an estate.) Before they had undertaker shops. The carpenters out there they had what you call pallbearer would dig the grave and the men around about the place there would build the coffin. And if the person died say today or tonight. They'd get together. And the women, if it were a woman, would go in there and bathe her and get her prepared. And the men built the coffin. They had to do it pretty soon because there was no embalming. In a day or two they had to go head on. So they'd take the person . . . Well, that night or day or until the time of the funeral everybody nearly on the place out there in that area would come and sit up all night long. Some men over yonder with a fire. They didn't have electric lights, lamps. Of course, some would be drinking and some telling jokes and all just to keep the other things going.

Since churches met only monthly, the worship service following a person's death would be the day of the eulogy. By the time it took place, the person might have been dead and buried a month.

Marriages were historically celebrated in ways orderly and disorderly. According to one account: "In front rode the bridegroom, on either side his groomsmen. The galloping, yelling, shooting crowd behind were his chosen friends, companions of boyhood and early manhood, to-day gathered from a radius of forty miles to pay him this tribute of friendship and esteem, according to a time-honored Wiregrass Georgia custom, known as 'running up' the bridegroom."A traditional dinner customarily followed the wedding ceremony at the bride's house. One historical account highlights the food:

> I must digress here to tell you something about our old-time weddings. Do you like chicken tart? If so, you ought to have lived in those days. Chicken pie or tart, as it was sometimes called, was the main dish at a wedding supper, which was served at the bride's home. A plenty of other good things were on hand, too. About everybody that knew of it went, invited or not invited. The ceremony was generally performed by a magistrate. I remember one, an uncle of the writer . . . , whose only fee was as many chicken gizzards as he could eat.

A full night of dancing to fiddle tunes followed the traditional meal. Furthermore, another dinner, called the "infair," customarily occurred the very next day at the home of the groom. "Here was gathered the big crowd of the night before, increased maybe by the older women and little children, and here was a bountiful supply of good things and more big eating. The latter, I suppose, took the place of a 'bridal tour.' "

Raucous revelry also occurred before dawn on the wedding night. Elsie Surber has furnished the following description:

> The "shivaree" [charivari] or serenade was a custom in those days, as it still is in some places. The neighbors got together and with all sorts of noise makers—pots, pans, guns—marched around the home of the newlyweds until the bridegroom gave them a "treat." This might be some sort of refreshment, whiskey or wine if the party were composed of men; or it might be that they simply wanted to be "invited in" for a party which they called a "play." If the bridegroom failed to comply with their request, they did something to him such as riding him on a rail or making him bring his bride to the door.

The richness and range of traditions suggest the wedding's significance for the larger community. Few marriages failed, because divorce was not an option. The words of the traditional wedding vow were applied literally. Community played an important role in helping relieve the tedium and

A fiddling contest at Landmark Park in Dothan, Alabama. Photo by Stephen Grauberger. Courtesy of the Alabama Center for Traditional Culture, Montgomery.

drudgery of subsistence living. Crises and days of celebration were opportunities for the community to bestow largesse that would later be returned in kind.

Occasions for recreation were frequent, taking place at the slightest provocation. People danced to the accompaniment of a fiddler and a fellow music maker who kept time by beating the straw—hitting a broom straw on the fiddle. William Rogers documented the introduction of the cakewalk into the region by African Americans. This social event later spread to the wider community. "Orange and pie eating contests were preludes to the main event, the cakewalk, and the evening closed with a dance for blacks. By 1891 cakewalks were so popular that it was claimed one was held every night in some part of the city." Cakes, then expensive and time-consuming to make, were a festive food and highly valued as a prize. Some regional festival organizers have revived the cakewalk for its traditional associations. Present-day festivals often seek to link the social realities of today with a community's heritage, thereby affording participants a sense of order and continuity.

CHAPTER 8

Festivals and Other Public Events

All societies take time out during the year for celebrations. Throughout the United States local festivals help communities to recenter by forcing them to focus on their common values and customs. These events, typically scheduled in the Wiregrass and elsewhere at predictable intervals, often attract masses of people.

Rural communities sometimes choose a theme for their festivals. Examples include the Honey Festival in Valdosta, Georgia; the Tomato Festival in Slocomb, Alabama; and the Panhandle Watermelon Festival in Chipley, Florida. In Wiregrass communities, as in other American towns, festivals fulfill a social function and also serve as fund raisers for the community. These institutionalized celebrations give the community a chance to look simultaneously backward at the past and forward toward the prospects for future growth.

Different Wiregrass towns have different festival themes. Each town selects an item of regional interest in which it takes pride. Residents then try to establish their town as "the capital" of some festival-related object. Some festivals are relatively recent inventions and have barely taken hold, such as Gnat Days in Camilla, Georgia, which commemorate the invisible line below which gnats multiply into dense populations and become pests. Morven, Georgia, has its Peach Festival. The Sweet Onion Festival in Glennville, Georgia, faces competition from its well-established neighbor, Vidalia. Even when towns' festivals have similar themes, however, the festivities have a distinctive local ambience. Georgia's Peanut Festival in Sylvester is inevitably smaller, less lucrative, and less publicized than the nationally renowned event held in Dothan, Alabama, but Sylvester's festival, being less commercial, is a more traditional celebration of the crop on which everyone's survival often depends. The more established festivals now have permanent grounds with down home names such as Climax's Chittling Barn, Sylvester's Possum Poke, and Pavo's Peacock Palace.

The Mayhaw Festival in Colquitt, Georgia, now about a dozen years old, is particularly distinctive, because the mayhaw fruit grows almost exclusively within Wiregrass Country and is ripe during only three weeks between the start of April and the end of May. Most local residents prize mayhaw jelly and butter, but few outsiders know about the fruit. Local color writer Arthur Powell has offered the best description. "It is made from a haw, of that reddish yellow color that one sees in pomegranate, hardly as big as the end of one's thumb." The trees flourish in lowland areas or even shallow ponds, though festival organizers once believed that they grew only in Colquitt County. An attempt is being made to market mayhaws commercially on a small scale, and mayhaw products can now be purchased at numerous outlets around the region.

E. W. Carswell said that mayhaws were "used much in the same manner of cranberry sauce as a flavor enhancer for other foods." Ophelia White of Sylvester, Georgia, an African American, learned about mayhaws from her grandmother and says that she has begun to elaborate upon her grandmother's teachings: "There was some that my grandmother didn't teach me. If my grandmother was still alive, I think that she would be fascinated at some things that I learned on my own and the way things are done now. She didn't know any of that because she had to do things the hard way."

According to White, "Mayhaws are not easy to get. You have to know where to get them from. For the past eight or nine years I had to go ten or twelve miles from here. Now I am truly blessed, this year on the way back I met a white friend: He said, 'Why in the world would you ride that far when you can just come on my farm?'" The products of White's kitchen include: fig preserves, pear preserves, peach preserves, peach jam, peach jelly, pear relish, apple relish, dill pickle, sweet pickle, apple jelly, blackberry jelly, jams and preserves, regular pickled peppers, and pickled watermelon rind. Her specialties are hot pear relish and, of course, the mayhaw jelly.

Some of the larger festivals have less to do with a specific crop, focus on some part of the animal kingdom, and have evolved from a theme into a concept. These festivals offer a spectacle and feature regional animals that were once important for the region's development. Festival-goers are invited to witness an event, whereas crop festivals often have no more than staged entertainment and the booths of vendors. Animal handling makes the concept festival both less predictable and more dramatic. Examples include Possum Day in Wausau, Florida; Mule Day in Calvary, Georgia; Swine Time in Climax, Georgia; and several rattlesnake roundups.

E. W. Carswell, in his work, "Possum Huntin' by Moonlight," describes the social meaning of such a hunting party. The emphasis here falls on "party." At one time, teenage youth "gathered to swap yarns while eating peanuts or chewing sugar cane taken from some nearby field. We'd sometimes sing, depending on whether our party included girls. Somehow, singing in the flickering light of a 'lighterd knot' fire on a chilly night wasn't much fun without girls." Possum hunting acquired importance during the depression, when the animal supplemented the diet of poverty-stricken families.

In later years, Wausau, Florida, began to celebrate the possum and erected a building called the Possum Palace for the purpose. Thirty years after the depression, the possum remains a durable theme for Wausau's Funday Festival. Southern gospel is the primary musical form. To build momentum, a week before the event, the festival organizers sponsor a gospel talent contest. The community also has its own Possum Concert Choir. The festival's main events occur annually on the first Saturday in August, Possum Day.

Concept festivals successfully compete with events conventionally called attractions. Although they may draw a relatively large outside following, for the most part these festivals involve neighborly forms of socializing. Like a reunion or homecoming, they are scheduled events that recur at the same time each year. Like the church ministries, singing conventions, and other community events, these festivals depend on a reciprocal support network. Residents from communities of similar size come together to engage in entertainment that reflects their shared cultural orientation.

Mule Day in Calvary, Georgia, is in many ways similar to Wausau's festival. It falls on the first Saturday in November. The mule is an animal intricately involved with the lives and the livelihoods of many local residents. Many families originally depended on a single mule with which to work the land. On Mule Day nearly a hundred "teamsters" descend on a community so small that it does not appear on many maps. Some mule owners arrive early in the week to swap mule stories and to engage in some mule trading. Mule traders, too, have a special place in regional lore as untrustworthy and unsavory characters.

Historically, the mule was considered to be a beloved companion. Carswell dedicated his book *Remembering Old Rhoady* to the family mule. Experienced mule aficionados often attribute their well-being and more to their mules. Carswell said that he was "indebted to [Old Rhoady] for additions to whatever strengths of character that I might lay claim." Like other pets, too, mules have sometimes been endowed with human dispositions and intellect. Carswell said that Old Rhoady "was mischievous at times, sometimes testing children by ignoring their commands. And she'd sometimes pretend that she didn't understand an order, and she'd outright ignore one if she thought she could get away with it. She knew she could intimidate some youngsters, but she was smart enough not to try such shenanigans with adults."

People became dependent on their mules, because in many cases their very livelihood hinged on the animals and their traits. In their personal experience narratives, many told how as children, individuals erred by not tending to the mule before going off to play. In most families, no one would be seated for dinner until the mule had been groomed and fed for the night.

The Mule Day festival site offers simultaneous stage performances, folk games, and over 500 vendors. These attractions remain secondary, however, to the serious business of mules. The parade features mainly equestrians, wagons, and mules—no floats, shriners, or even a beauty contest—with prizes awarded in several categories. The mule drivers spend most of the day in open competition at the mule show. Prizes are awarded for the best plow mule or cotton mule under command, and there are events devoted to particular tasks, such as log pulling. Because mules are stubborn, success depends on the relationship between the animal and its handler.

With the advent of Mule Day, community leaders open up their town to a crowd looking mainly for the marketplace. Festival organizers sell cane syrup cooked by the old-time mule-operated mill and bottled on the "Mule Day" grounds. Historically, sugarcane was one of the best cash crops. Moreover, cane grinding supplied Wiregrass Country with sweetener. Syrup making began in the late fall, continued until Christmas, and involved the entire family. According to one family history, "They would only make a barrel and a half of syrup in a day. The cane was ground by a mule-pulled mill. The family would arise at four o'clock in the morning for breakfast and would be ready to go to work at sunrise; they would work until sundown."

Most families made such massive quantities that they were able to use syrup liberally. Owen Wrice remembered that his African American family "would grind out two or three barrels a year, and each of us had our own gallon of syrup. We wouldn't bother nobodies. We made sweet water, we sopped syrup, we made syrup sandwiches anyway that you could deal with that syrup." A member of another family said, "I recall my daddy mixing water and cane syrup to drink for a quick 'pick up' of energy." There was even a popular saying: "When its syrup making time, ya'll come!" Carswell said, "My father, who had some Puritanical leanings, fed this by-product of his syrup mill to our hogs. This kept it from being used for sinful purposes. And the hogs were glad."

Some residents, however, did use the syrup for "sinful purposes," namely a popular form of moonshine called cane buck. Although it was illegal, moonshine served as a form of legal tender and supplemented incomes as social security does today. According to one local story: "a woman who

Sugarcane being processed into syrup. Photo courtesy of Vanishing Georgia, Georgia Department of Archives and History, Atlanta.

had lost her husband was given five gallons of moonshine by the church committee to 'help her make a crop.' " According to Carswell, residents considered moonshining a respectable sideline. Silas Cotton, a local hero, reportedly "sold no 'shine before its time": "Silas was a religious character who strictly observed the Sabbath and gave one-tenth of his gross earnings to the church."

The moonshiners guarded their recipes and developed an efficient, waste-free system of production. Ophelia White recalled her father's distillery:

> As I told you earlier, we had our own cane. You would grind the cane and make the syrup and what they call the skimming off of it that went over into a wooden barrel. . . . they would get those sixty gallon barrels of what they called cane skimmings and that would stay there and sour. They would put a burlap bag that was better known then as croker bag over it. And they would put a piece of wire around the top, that was to keep insects out of it. And they would let it stay there until it just would start to bubble up. And you could smell it. I don't know why they didn't just stay in jail for it because, if you went along there, you could smell that stuff. You knew something was going on and it would stay there maybe probably a week or two until it got just ripe.

A moonshine still about to be confiscated, early 1900s. Photo courtesy of Vanishing Georgia, Georgia Department of Archives and History, Atlanta.

Then, he would go out there, and they would skim the top off and he would take a lard can which was . . . I think they called it a forty-five pound can and that was what he would put the . . . they called it buck and that is what they put the buck in that can. He took a pipe (now they use copper), but it wasn't a copper pipe that he would put in—it was more just a regular galvanized-type pipe that you could buy at your hardware stores. He would take that pipe and put it into that can. And when he put it into the can, they would take a trough that was made of boards. And they would make the trough of boards, and it would be made in like . . . Well, you would hold your hand like this and at the end of it there would be boards on the end that would hold it together. They would run a pipe all the way through down the bottom of it because it would lay right on top of where he put those boards together. And they would put water in that trough (that was to keep the pipe cool). And as he put the can over a slow burning fire, the steam was what would come up and make the liquor come out. And when it come out, it's clear because when you see it over here it is all dull and . . . Have you seen cane juice? That's what it looks like; but by the time it come out, it is just as clear as water. And he would let it run. The first that would come off, he would call it "low wine"—the first that's coming off. But then he would run off about a quart of that that they called low wine, and you wouldn't use that because that didn't go into your good liquor. Then, comes your good liquor.

And if you was in here cooking it, you could smell it . . . oh gosh . . . if the wind caught it just right, you could smell it a block away. But like I say, I don't know why they didn't stay in jail because they was doing what it took to keep them in there. But he was the main . . . everybody called him . . . he was the main bootlegger there so he would cook it off for uh . . . several people. He would do it for them.

Once he get it cooked off, then what was left that wasn't any good. We had hogs so he would just take that and mix corn with it and set it out there. He could feed it to the hogs in two or three days because, if you gave it to them right then, your hogs would get drunk from it. You'd go out there and have a pen full of hogs just laying out there just as high as a kite. So you would have to wait until it swells that corn up, and it gets soft. Then, you know that it has already absorbed the alcohol into the corn so that means that it broke down the quantity of alcohol that was in there. Then, you could give it to your hogs. And then you could also take it, and you could use corn like that and put it in your buck as they called it in the bottom of that barrel where the cane skimmings are. And, I guess, then you would consider that your 100 proof liquor because then you had some really strong alcohol.

In some places moonshining was so accepted that no effort was made to conceal it. Wiregrass festivals build upon such reminiscences.

Climax, Georgia, with a population of approximately 500, was named for its location at the highest point on the Seaboard Coast Line Railroad between Montgomery and Savannah and calls itself the "Home of Swine Time." Its festival takes place on the Saturday following Thanksgiving more or less during the traditional hog-killing season.

Almost all of the festival's events focus on swine. Some activities carry over from the past; others are more recent in origin. They include contests such as Best Dressed Pig, Kiss the Pig, Chitterlin' Eating, Hog Imitations, Hog Calling, and the Greasy Pig Chase. There is also a competitive hog show, evidence that swine raising is still a way of life for many of the participants. Festival literature speaks of the days when hogs roamed the earth in yokes, wooden or metal restraints attached to their necks in order to protect farmers' gardens and fields. The celebration reflects affection for the animal and its by-products, which were once necessary for everyday survival.

Many Wiregrass residents lament their inability nowadays to acquire freshly butchered meats. Olin Pope, a white resident of Barwick, Georgia, said, "I wish that I had some of it [fresh meat] now. . . . The government got into it and the state. You can't have it now. It [store bought meats] ain't fit to eat. I was raised on it. . . . It was cured. You cured it with salt and you washed it off with salt and you put cloves and honey, black pepper and red pepper on it to give it that seasoning and mixed it with syrup and you hung it up and smoked it." Governmental forces are often blamed for disrupting an important link with the past. It is illegal today to butcher and to eat uninspected meat.

Although some people hated hog-killing time, which usually occurred on the first cold day of the season, they remember the process in vivid detail. The hog's liver and lights (lungs) were cooked and eaten early in the hog-killing festivities. People sometimes walked miles to deliver packages of meat to family friends. As the saying goes, "Farmers lived well but were cash poor." They gave generously of themselves and of their resources. Most adults also vividly remember the preparation of sausages and meats. Ophelia White reminisced:

> My grandfather knew how to preserve this stuff. . . . we had sausage that would be from one time of killing the hog to the next time. Because he smoked it. . . . what they would call then fresh was when they would take the meat out and cook it down to make the lard out of (which now we know not to touch). Then, we were making crackling. While it was hot, they would take those sausages and you put them over in the can where your lard was going, and you pour that hot lard in there on them, in which that cooked that sausage in there. And so whenever you wanted a fresh sausage that was it. . . . Back in those times, it kept real good.

Olin Pope and others recalled the important function played by wiregrass in their everyday domestic lives. "We used to hang meat with it" in the smokehouse.

In the tobacco region, Owen Wrice said, "We take that beef and slice it and hang it on tobacco sticks in the smokehouse and dried it and we took some of it and put it in one of those cans and put meal in it and keep it that way." Wrice's family used another method to preserve sausage: "We make those sausages and we'd cook those crackling out and we take those sausages. We curl them around in that can that you put lard in and we cooked that crackling out and you'd take that lard and dip it out and pour it on that sausage and cook that sausage. That's what we did to keep that fresh sausage."

Barbecue has a tradition all its own. Many visitors travel the South sampling different varieties. Communities everywhere now hold contests. In the South, grilled meat has long been a part of every festive gathering and, with roadside restaurants, has become available any day of the week. Richardson's Pit Bar-B-Que on Old Highway 84 in Iron City, Georgia, is widely acclaimed. The owner's stepson reported, "We had airplanes to stop a couple of times." Helicopters stop, too. Because Richardson's is located next to a railroad track, train crews are regular customers, as are truckers. The

A rattlesnake roundup in Fitzgerald, Georgia, 1974. Photo courtesy of
Vanishing Georgia, Georgia Department of Archives and History, Atlanta.

owners say that their barbecue is prepared "the old-fashioned way—meat
on the bone." Richardson's concession stand is a mainstay at several area
festivals.

Rattlesnake roundups take place in several regions. Claxton, Georgia;
Fitzgerald, Georgia; Whigham, Georgia; and Opp, Alabama, all feature annual roundups, although Opp calls its event a "rodeo." At these events,
regardless of the name, awards are given to the contestants who round up
the most eastern diamondback rattlesnakes (sometimes hundreds) or the
heaviest specimen. These festivals thus serve as a way of controlling the
snake population. Many people believe that the snakes proliferated when
people ceased to burn the woods. It is perhaps not accidental that the festivals became popular in the 1960s, when laws were enacted to prohibit un-
controlled burning.

Every year, as many as 30,000 people attend the parade and festival in
Whigham, Georgia (population 500). Some vendors offer food or arts and
crafts, but snake handling is clearly the main event. The judging process
generally transfixes the thrill-seeking crowd. After the parade, a snake handler spends the entire day tallying entries while spectators watch his every
movement. Snakes arrive in all sorts of containers many of which reflect
no mean ingenuity on the part of their makers. Hundreds of rattlers (and

a cottonmouth or two) go on display, and a snake specialist milks each snake of its venom. After the festival the snakes are shipped to Arizona, where they are allegedly used for research.

In contrast, Claxton's Rattlesnake Roundup promotes its event as "the beauty with the beasts" competition. This festival was created as a result of a snakebite in the community. Instead of being staged outdoors, as in Whigham, the main events take place in a tobacco warehouse, where snakes and beauties are judged simultaneously. Judging of the snake competition occurs at the same time as the crowning of the roundup queen. Women and serpents separately and in combination are of course traditionally powerful biblical symbols.

Beauty pageants, the cornerstone of most community-based festivals in the Wiregrass, are a way of life for many young girls. In most instances, without a pageant, there would be no festival or parade. These are not parades in the classic sense, often lacking marching bands or floats, but usually involve motorcades transporting beauties that lead the masses to the festival grounds. The Claxton Rattlesnake Roundup Parade, for example, features over a dozen pageant queens, bearing titles such as Miss Gum Spirit and Turpentine, Miss Georgia Sweet Onion, Miss Liberty County, Miss Coastal Georgia, Miss Pinewood Christian Academy, and Miss Forestry Queen.

These pageants respond to locally intense interest in regional, state, and national competitions. Small-town pageants in Wiregrass Country seldom lead contestants to the Miss America contest, and indeed only a select few, such as the peanut festival in Dothan, even qualify the winners on the state level. Nonetheless, the pageants teach young women to vie for honors and give them a sophistication that they would otherwise miss, growing up in a typical Wiregrass community. By competing, and even by participating in local parades, they earn community recognition and perhaps greater self-confidence.

Whether someone wins the title or loses, the contestant acts as a community volunteer. She has joined a legion of women who donate time and energy, some of whom eventually develop careers raising money for worthwhile causes. To enter, each contestant must pay a minimum sponsorship fee, and she is encouraged to raise extra money by participating in an additional scholarship or prize competition. The typical Wiregrass pageant entails no talent show, no platform, and no questioning. Although contestants usually speak only a few lines of introduction, some crop festivals require their contestants to be knowledgeable about the product that they will represent. Ordinarily the only requirement is that contestants demonstrate a self-possession that will reflect favorably upon their community.

Many pageant contestants initially competed in a Junior Miss, Little

The beauty queen at an annual convention of the American Turpentine Farmers Association, c. 1954. Photo courtesy of Georgia Agrirama, Tifton.

Miss, Wee Miss, or even Diaper Princess pageant. These girls learn at tender ages how capricious society can be. In children's competitions, judges usually select a winner on the basis of their party dress alone. Increasingly, young boys compete to be crowned kings. Even high school homecoming titles reach into the elementary and middle schools for contestants. Although few local pageants require a display of talent, youngsters often enroll in dance or gymnastic schools to help them with their presentation style. For today's young people, many of whom are veteran contestants by their senior year in high school, pageantry has become a mediating structure in their lives.

Parades in Wiregrass Country are minute in comparison with those seen on television. These processions often require less than a half hour to view. Mostly linear, they have different beginning and ending points and cover a route of at most a few city blocks. Like the circus parades of the past, and like barnstorming baseball league parades, these serve to introduce the main event. Nonetheless, they celebrate, create, and communicate the fact of community. Community participation is consequently essential, and these parades deliver. On an immediate level, they promote an intense experience that breaks down community barriers. Annually, furthermore, they represent a time of renewal.

Annual festivals recreate the marketplaces of the past. They give local businesses a financial boost and offer community folk, churches, and organizations a chance to act as entrepreneurs. At times they attract more vendors than residents. Such markets encourage creativity while also helping to improve the quality of life. Far from sounding the death knell for folk art, the festival offers a lifeline—space for every representative of the community.

Crop festivals are not synonymous with food festivals. Food of course plays a significant role in festivals, but the featured produce is seldom prepared as part of the festival fare or made the subject of cooking contests. Instead, food vendors offer varied dishes, everything from the everyday southern cuisine, sold by local churches and auxiliaries, to cotton candy, funnel cakes, and corndogs, sold by outside vendors.

Festivals are perhaps the closest modern equivalent to firemen's musters, court week, and tobacco or cotton market days of the past. The firemen's musters, for instance, began with the formation of volunteer fire companies in the 1870s. Towns began to compete against one another, and the contests, which helped build firefighting skills, attracted local interest. The competition was usually preceded by a parade of firemen in fancy and artistic uniforms. African Americans maintained separate volunteer units. One local historian comments, "These Negro fire-companies were credited by the Quitman newspapers on more than one occasion for preventing the spread of fires through their heroic efforts." In the past, any event that brought people together soon became a festive occasion. Civic and business activities, such as court sessions or farmers' market days, all gave rise to some type of celebration.

Today's crop festivals differ from the county fairs of the past, which involved competitions in each agricultural realm. Competition helped reward workers for their labors. Community leaders recognized that county fairs stimulated business as much as did routine election days and market days. In 1906, Bulloch County, Georgia, began to consider instituting a fair as a promotional tool. An editorial in the *Statesboro News* asked, "Why Not Have a County Fair?" "It would cause rivalry among the farmers, for each one would try to grow a finer crop or have finer stock than his neighbor. It would help the town, for the merchants would profit much from the large crowds who usually attend fairs. It would help them so much that they could afford to offer prizes for the best exhibits and the finest stock."

Most of today's community festivals arose after the 1960s. Integration seems to have disrupted the flow of these county fairs. Like everything else in the Jim Crow South, the county fairs were segregated. Today most festivals attempt some multicultural diversity. Wherever several groups are represented, their constituent communities turn out en masse.

Some celebrations, like the River Front Festival in Geneva, Alabama, extol the most visible local resource. Others, such as Old South Day in Ochlocknee, Georgia, celebrate the past in general. Wildfest, in Pelham, Georgia, cannot readily be defined. While these festivals seek to benefit from tourism, they have in common a commitment to place and to community, an extension of the old system of reciprocity.

More than pageants or festivals, however, high school football teams probably serve as the region's best cultural markers today. Football games have, since the 1940s, become a core ritual around which most communities now organize their lives. Football builds on tradition. It promotes local loyalty and provides an outlet for competitiveness. The year Charlie Ward won the Heisman trophy, his high school won the state championship playing against another school from his hometown. Wiregrass high schools, which have consolidated, in the tristate region regularly win a disproportionate share of state championships in all divisions. Highway 84 is considered the measuring stick for high school football in Georgia, because schools along it consistently win the championship. College recruiters take Highway 84 when they select potential players.

Football has an avid following throughout the South, but winning has a particular tradition in Wiregrass Country. For instance, Coach Ralph Jones of Cairo High School in Georgia attributed the spirit at his school to "the interest that their brothers played, their daddies played, and their uncles played, and it meant a lot to them." The oral tradition inherited by each new generation encompasses highlights from the past victorious seasons.

As Coach Jones observed, "Everybody has something to rally around, you know. No matter what color you are. No matter how much money you got. . . . It's something that's on Friday . . . The town just kinda looks for the Friday night football game. And say Cairo's playing and who they're playing. It's a sense of pride, and I just think it something that everybody forget about their problems and they all just kinda get behind something, and that's the high school team." The booster clubs rival those of the college teams. The hometown crowd travels to away games and tailgates, with enthusiasm like that shown at religious camp meetings in the past. During the playoff games on Saturday nights, Bibles frequently appear in the stand. Fans bring them not to influence the outcome of the game but to prepare for Sunday school lessons. Winning is often taken for granted.

On the regular Friday night before football games, people mill about the stadium, greeting friends, seeing, and being seen. Fans spread gossip and chat throughout the game. The weather in the region remains warm for most of the season, adding to the game's appeal. Although a woman is overheard declaring, "I enjoy football when its not hot and ain't raining," many fans are hardy. Even in the driving rain, they will turn out.

When the stadium fills up, electricity builds in the stands. Stylized cheers are relatively commonplace, and staunch fans bring cowbells and jugs as noisemakers. Much of the student body may participate in the activities on game night. At Cairo High School, for example, the student body numbers 1,200 students, and the band has 250 members. The coach says, "You got that girl out there . . . a majorette for that band and your family is going. That granddaddy's going to come and watch that granddaughter." Slogans decorate the stadium, and the players charge through a paper gauntlet before every game. The hoopla reserved for homecoming games nationally appears at every game during the Wiregrass football season.

Certain rituals, pranks, and hijinks are part of the game, too. Besides mission statements, special tee shirts, and secret societies, psychological ploys are devised to motivate the players. For example, a gold dot is sometimes placed on players' watches to promote a feeling of solidarity throughout the day. Traditional rivalries with neighboring schools involve ritual pranks. Cairo High School's team, known as the Syrupmakers, used to be accused of pouring syrup on the mascot of a rival team. Other past pranks include sending black flowers, a casket, or woman's underwear to the other team.

The long-standing rivalry between Cairo and Thomasville High School remains intense. Since the 1950s, the two schools have awarded a syrup pitcher to the winner after the season game. Cairo fans say, "Cairo has to have it because it's ours."

As in the past, Wiregrass communities find ways to celebrate and to renew community bonds. With the demise of singing schools and the old singing conventions, there would be nothing to equal the market days and court weeks of the past without community-based festivals or sports events. Wiregrass towns have many of the same problems as the larger American cities, whose resources they lack. What Wiregrass communities have in abundance, however, is the same ingenuity of their ancestors.

CHAPTER 9

Outdoor Activities

The typical Wiregrass resident values outdoor life almost as strongly as religious life. With its many creeks and streams and pristine forests, Wiregrass Country is ideal for both hunting and fishing, activities that people pursue for pleasure alone or in small groups. According to Dave Mathis, "The best time to go fishing is when you have a pole, the hooks, the bait, and the gasoline in your car to get you there"—in short, almost anytime you feel like it.

Many ancestors relied on hunting and fishing as subsistence activities. As historian William Rogers has noted, "Expeditions combining the two sports were not rare, and social affairs were often held in conjunction with hunting or, more often, fishing outings." Hunting parties formed during the celebration of holidays such as Thanksgiving and Christmas. In the warmer months, fish fries dominated the scene. One enthusiast recalled:

> The men would go fishin', you know and go out to some—like up to Whiddon Mill or some lake somewhere, or some creek, and they would go and fish, may be a day in advance. And camp out that night. Then the women and the children would go join them the next day, and they would of course take food, but . . . they would have fish fries. They then did the cooking. They'd gather up somewhere on the creek or near that pond and they'd all go and have fish fry, you know, and everybody enjoyed it. That was through the week, any day through the week. You didn't go fishin' on Sunday. That was a no-no! No one would fish on Sunday.

Although Sundays were traditionally off limits, people fished and hunted at all other times, including nighttime. Young people enjoyed nocturnal hunting for possums and deer. J. L. Herring described the "Old Time Fire-Hunt": "The boys had made up the hunt the night before, and during the day's plowing laid their plans. One quit work before night to get a supply of fat splinters, the other requisitioned the frying-pan without Mother's consent and pieced out the handle with a stick of wood. After supper at early candle-light they started." The light from a torch would immobilize a hapless deer, making it easy prey. Surreptitious activity added excitement and a sense of danger. When women were present, young men preferred possum hunting. The young people could court while the hunting dogs trailed and treed the game. Also, tradition dictated that, when a boy shot his first deer, the community of hunters would cut off his shirttail to initiate him into the sport.

Many different types of game are hunted in the Wiregrass: ducks, doves, turkeys, quails, and even crows. Hunters enjoy telling stories about their prey, which is endowed with human attributes. E. W. Carswell recalled crow-hunting season: "Crows seem to consider it great sport to outwit people. And they go about it gleefully, seeming to find the task so easy that it's hilariously funny to them. That's why they've probably laughed themselves hoarse after reading about Florida's crow hunting season. They're going to have themselves some fun."

Some hunters introduced fictitious animals into the landscape. For instance, "snipe hunting" has as much to do with joking behavior and pranks as with an actual chase. A researcher on the South Georgia Folklife Project reported: "Roberts asked if I've ever been snipe-hunting. . . . Mrs. Stokes, I think it was, said that they were described to her as small furry animals a little like rabbits whose fur could be sold. You tapped the ground and said, 'Here, snipe—here, snipe.' " Hunting expeditions have their own special language, home brew, and tales of guns, dogs, and past exploits.

Hunters like to stalk their quarry, and the hunt for each entails collective rules of sportsmanship. Dove shoots, for example, developed into a team competition in the early 1890s. Accordingly, "True sportsmen believed the birds should be given a sporting chance and shot only in flight, never on the ground or at rest. Some refused to deliberately bait fields, utilizing the peanut or corn fields after harvest for their dove shoots. These, too, in a sense were baited fields." Doves represented popular game birds and in competition were killed by the hundreds.

Animals with a special place in the life of the hunter often become the subject of tall tales. According to folklorist Tad Tuleja, "Turkey hunting has been variously defined as an addiction, an affliction, an art closely paralleling black magic or voodoo, an excuse for seclusion and plain damn foolishness." The wild turkey has been characterized as stupid but wary to a fault, traits that do not make it easy prey but perhaps increase its desirability. For instance, "Uncle Sam went turkey hunting—brought only one shot—forgot his lead balls. Saw five turkeys on a limb—split it—feet went down in a crack and caught them—carried them all home on the limb. Worst thing that ever happened was down in a lime sink—turkey in tree over him, rattlesnake at his feet, just behind him, an alligator, ducks on one side, something else—gun shot at the deer, trigger choked rattler, hammer got turkey, one barrel got quail, other got ducks, something got the gator."

The quail, however, and not the turkey, is the quintessential game bird in Wiregrass Country. The remaining stands of wiregrass owe their existence largely to the efforts made to protect this game bird. William Rogers reported various folk beliefs that quail could control their scent, shield themselves by grasping leaves in flight, and call to one another to signal a warning to nearby nests.

Many northern industrialists invested in quail hunting plantations within the Wiregrass region after the Civil War, especially in areas adjacent to Thomasville, Georgia. These large estates—northern woodland hunting plantations—replaced the cotton-growing plantations that had dotted the land almost a hundred years earlier. According to Rogers, "The sports, particularly hunting, proved lasting attractions for Northern visitors long after the vogue of breathing pine-scented air was past." The Northerners ignored local customs and imported their accustomed lifestyle when they visited the sites they had purchased. They transformed Thomasville, Georgia, into a resort town by coming to "take the cure." They considered the Piney Woods restorative, so they lived in the region from October through March. The typical northern enthusiasts were business moguls such as the Woodruff family of Coca-Cola fame, who owned Ichuaway, a prototypical plantation on the periphery of the Wiregrass region.

These so-called northern plantations are held in special regard by the African Americans who were reared on them and whose parents made up the plantation workforce. The properties were self-contained: the plantation workers constructed the roads and maintained the buildings. Pebble Hills employed about sixty families who lived on the plantation. Some workers rented a one-horse farm for fifty dollars a year—that is, a dollar an acre. In essence, they earned a salary and worked on shares, which means that they paid out a half-share annually for all they produced on the land they rented. The plantations were so large, and the buildings so numerous, that it took painters much of the season to whitewash them all.

The dairy workers supplied the milk products for both the household and the workers alike. Dog trainers filled the highest echelon of the labor force, however. It was not uncommon for a bird dog to cover twenty or twenty-five miles during a day of quail hunting. Their trainers therefore had to condition them with a special diet and a strenuous exercise regimen. Because of their importance, the dogs had their own cooks and a separate kitchen for the preparation of their food.

The descendants of the plantation workers often feel that their parents' labor was not exploited. The northern families built private schools and churches for their workers and employed a private nurse for their families. Also, on most plantations, the owners excused their employees' wives and children from work and thereby encouraged the formation of patriarchal families. On "Pay Saturday," workers labored half a day, whereas "Blank Saturday" was just like any other working day.

On Pay Saturday, everybody went to town. A truck belonging to the owners usually took the workers to town and brought them back with their groceries. In town, stores remained open until 10:00 p.m. Because their parents earned dependable salaries, most significantly during the depression, descendants today attribute their professional success in part to the enlightened attitudes of these northern plantation owners, who encouraged their education.

The northerners brought their own twist to the plantation system. The paternalism that they practiced fostered greater autonomy rather than dependency. Racism, however, was no less pervasive. The owners typically hired white southerners as "the experts" to act as superintendents and to oversee the workers.

Tommie Gabriel of Thomas County, Georgia, recalled that a superintendent expelled his family from Pebble Hill because his father overstepped the bounds of southern convention. In 1926, Miami was experiencing a building boom and recruited laborers. Instead of earning $1.75 per day on the plantation, workers could get $3.00 or $4.00 a day working in Miami. Out of season, the hands therefore surreptitiously left the plantation to work elsewhere, hoping to come back before their employers had returned. Gabriel commented that his "father came back in a '26 Ford. We were not going to be able to stay there. The foreman said that we were creating a disturbance."

Gabriel states that his father had taken the precaution of buying a home and had already considered moving before another planting season arrived. Evidently, the owners employed the superintendents to act as middlemen and to run interference when southern mores were being challenged. According to southern custom, African Americans were forbidden from enjoying greater affluence than the poorest of their white neighbors. After surveying the available options, workers usually chose the job security and protection that laboring on northern plantations offered.

Mark Hanna, an industrialist, and his family were the first northerners to own a plantation in the Thomasville area. In time, most of the nearby owners came to be relatives of the Hannas. On Pebble Hill, the best-known site, single African American women lived in a residence hall called the

Waldorf. The workers also had access to the Showboat, a theater on Melrose Plantation that showed first-run films such as *Gone with the Wind.*

Festive occasions provided the survivors of these plantations with pleasant memories. Traditionally, several plantations formed a social unit, and each was responsible for hosting Fourth of July, Easter, or Emancipation Day celebrations. For instance, Sinkola Plantation might host the Fourth of July celebration, Winnstead Plantation the Emancipation Day observance, and Pebble Hill the Easter event. These events were always elaborate. For the Fourth of July, the people cooked goat, deer, and pigs throughout the night. The plantations formed their own baseball teams, complete with uniforms, umpires, and the best equipment. At Easter, Pansy Poe (Elisabeth Ireland) of Pebble Hill held an Easter egg hunt with prize eggs. At these hunts, the children formed into a basket brigade so that everyone could receive treats. According to surviving accounts, Pansy Poe was tireless in her devotion to her employees. Willie Johnson of Thomas County, Georgia, a one-time resident, insisted that Poe "knew everybody on her place. She didn't know of them; she knew them." At Christmas, her gifts included brand new clothing, fabric, dolls, wagons, tricycles, and fruit.

The hunting practiced on the northern plantations represented upper-class recreation. Hunters from around the world came to hunt the bobwhite quail, considered one of the most challenging of game birds. A professional team of hunters included the plantation manager, the dog trainer, at least three scouts, and a wagon driver. Guests could ride horseback or, if they preferred, in a magnificent wagon drawn by two well-groomed draft horses. The workers were charged with ensuring that the hunters experienced the ultimate in quail hunting. During the hunt, usually six trained bird dogs pointed twenty-one coveys of wild, native bobwhite quail. A covey may have up to twenty-five quail, but shooters might be limited to only four birds per covey. They could shoot the limit on the covey rise, and they could also hunt single birds that scattered.

The hunting season abounded with rituals, with the best saved for last. According to author Charles Elliott:

> On the last day of the quail season our head Negro "made a narration" to the tenants giving them permission to "put out the fire," which, the buildings and fences having already been raked around, they promptly did, "putting the fire" to everything else that would burn. That night, on every hand, lines of flames crept or raced across the fields, flickering through pine woods, here and there flaring high over the heavier clumps of weeds, accompanied by cracklings of brush, bands like pistol shots, and clouds of eye- and nose-stinging smoke.

The finale incorporated a controlled burning that marked not merely the end of one season but preparation for those to come.

Quail season attracted many celebrities, including President Dwight Eisenhower, to the region's hunting plantations. Photo courtesy of the Thomas County Historical Museum.

As this account of the hunt suggests, hunting dogs were cherished possessions. Historian Ted Ownby has commented, "Though many could not afford horses, virtually all Southern rural families in the late nineteenth and twentieth centuries owned dogs." Hunters developed preferences for different breeds. Some fancied hounds over bird dogs. The kennels of the elite commonly housed pointers and setters. Rogers commented: "It is doubtful that in many areas the death of a coon and possum dog would have rated an editorial. Yet when Steve Williams's 'Old Rat' died in 1888 the *Times* noted, 'He was a regular George Washington, and when he opened,' nothing remained but to decide who should tote the 'possums.'" Dog cemeteries abound in the South.

Hunting dogs often play a central role in the prose narratives that hunters tell. On August 12, 1977, Dave Stanley recorded the following story at the home of Luther A. Bailey (sometimes known as "Lying" Bailey) south of Sycamore in Turner County, Georgia:

> You talking about hunting—you don't know nothing about these coons, do you? . . . . Well they are mighty fast, when the first mile or two or three miles, you jump one. You just about the fastest thing on foot there is till they find a tree.

I had one of the best coon dogs going across them woods you ever saw. And he struck his durn coon and that coon went right out and across the open field. And they just looked like he was just going, going to catch that coon every minute. He was just biting at him. Woof, woof. And he quit. And never did bark no more.

I took my lantern and went out across there, see could I find him, find out what was wrong. That dog was laying out there dead. And do you know—that coon was running so fast until them rings on his tail slipped off from his tail and went over the dog's neck and choked him to death.

As with snipe hunting, such tall tales initiate outsiders to the sport and the sportsmen. The following prose narrative was given to a folklorist assumed to be unfamiliar with the motifs:

Cothran: What about dogs? D'you have any hunting dogs?

Griffis: Ohh, yeah, I got some tur'ble good deer dogs. I useta coon hunt a lot, but I don't have any coon dogs now. I useta have a good un, he 'as often treein' five an' six coons up one tree; but I went to 'im one day where 'e's treed up a large, tall tree wi'long branches on it. I looked up that tree an' it was jus' coons, coons, all over that tree. I started at top t' shooting 'em out. When I got down t' the bottom, my pile o' coons was higher than the tree, an' the last un I shot had t' fall ninety foot straight up t' be on top.

The excitement and dangers that hunters encountered during the hunt entered into their personal experience narratives. Some tales grew incrementally into tall tales, whereas others remain the factual, relatively straightforward tales of everyday life.

Expert hunters often learn to communicate with their hounds. Numerous accounts of expeditions highlight communication between man and beast, so that the dogs seem almost human. Carswell related an incident that he attributed to Earnest J. Cox, Jr., a neighbor. Puzzled by his dog's silence while chasing a fox, Mr. Cox retraced his dog's path later: "That sly fox was leading the hound through a posted field, hoping the dog would obey the 'no hunting' signs or get himself in trouble with the owner. But the dog was too smart to get caught in that trap. He simply stopped baying while chasing the fox across that posted field."

Hunters also developed strong preferences regarding the use of their dogs. Kenny Foy said, "I like to hunt with four or five hounds, or at least enough to form a quartet. . . . A well-balanced pack of hounds will harmonize beautifully, with the bass, tenor, soprano, alto and sometimes baritone voices, coming into play with remarkable clarity and timing."

Barking dogs signify that the chase is on—the highlight of any hunt. Carolyn Chason of Grady County, Georgia, recalled: "My dad enjoyed quail hunting, and he enjoyed deer hunting. The type of deer hunting that he did at that point was a group activity in which they had the dogs. The dogs would chase and run the deer. And . . . they would train the dogs. They would make noises when they saw the deer and the hunters would each have a stance, only they would have a spot. And they would probably . . . My dad would always say 'the greatest fun was just hearing the dogs bark.' " The barks of dogs indicated their progress as they tracked their prey. In addition, fox and coon hunters carried hunter's horns made from conch shells and the horns of long-horned bulls or rams.

Much of the hunting in Wiregrass Country added variety to the residents' diet. Many hunters, however, never acquired a taste for certain meats. Carolyn Chason said, "My father would always—when asked by an outsider, if he enjoyed venison—he always say, 'Yes, it's very delicious.' If you put some on the table he would pass it right by." Their passion for hunting reflected more than appetite, of course. According to Ownby, "For an upcountry South Carolina man at the turn of the century, opossum hunting 'gave you a wild feeling of being free, of standing alone against darkness and all the forces that bound and cramped you.' " Landowners also profited from the sport because they were able to let someone "buy up" the hunting rights to their property rather than use it for row crops.

Commentators offered various explanations for the appeal of hunting to the masculine psyche. Ownby ascribed a frontier mentality to the men who slaughtered their prey before the advent of more stringent gaming laws. "Men frequently recalled special hunts—usually those involving particular feats of marksmanship or cunning—as being among the most exciting and memorable moments of their lives." For boys, learning to hunt was a rite of passage that secured their place in masculine society.

According to Bertram Wyatt-Brown, "About some things mothers and wives were to be obeyed, but on the muster field and in hunting camp, never." Many men seem to have used hunting to subvert the status quo as mediated by religion and women. "Hunting, unlike most other male recreations, was a thoroughly respectable activity that had the full approval of churchmen, wives, and mothers, but it was also an outlet for the self-assertiveness and self-indulgence that had long constituted an important feature of Southern male culture."

Hunting clearly fell within a male precinct, and outside the elite class (in which women were known to test the boundaries of propriety), women seldom took part. When it came to entertainment or assistance after the hunt, however, women played a more prominent role. Nowadays, many people have lost interest in hunting. As Ophelia White of Sylvester, Georgia, remarked: "We grew up eating stuff like that, and it comes a time in your life to say there is no need to kill something like that."

Hunters in Wiregrass Country examine their prey. Photo courtesy of Vanishing Georgia, Georgia Department of Archives and History, Atlanta.

Fishing has traditionally been a more universal pastime, both in the South in general and in Wiregrass Country in particular. Wiregrass residents will stake out almost any available body of water so that they can "drown worms." Fishing is a so-called poor man's sport and can be pursued with the expenditure of relatively little energy. Then too, the fisherman who returns home without a catch can always talk about "the one that got away." The following narrative is representative: "One man says he caught a fish 4½ feet long. Other says he caught a lantern that was lit. First protested. Second said that if the first would take a foot off the fish, he'd blow the lantern out." Local newspapers, perhaps anticipating skeptics, routinely publish photographs showing the catch at area lakes and ponds.

Fishing today seems hardly less prevalent than in the past. Reportedly, "Thomas countians needed little provocation to go fishing. A report that the red bellies or red gills or jackfish were biting would send people to the Ochlocknee in such numbers 'the paths are as big as the wagon roads.' "

People generally say that a competent fishermen can both smell the fish and read the signs of a catch. For those who know that the universe is not silent, the fish can be abundant. Carswell explained the meaning of the vernacular phrase, "A bed of Bream," a regional favorite:

> The "beds" were clear places, often on a sandy lake or stream bottom, where the fish were spawning. . . . It was not difficult to catch them while polefishing

at such times and places, either because the fish were hungry or because they resented intrusions and would bite at anything that seemed to threaten the sanctity of their bedroom. I'm not sure the phases of the moon influenced the bedding or biting processes, but I seem to recall that I usually had good fishing luck during a growing or full moon.

The most competent fishermen can tell by time of day, weather, the moon, and so forth when the fish will be biting. Sometimes their information can be quite specific. C. L. Talley used to say, "Go catfishing three days before the full moon. If cows are under a tree, don't fish. If they're grazing go." People who go by the moon will say, "Well, you ought to catch 13 fish this year—one every full moon—that's what you catch, isn't it?" One informant maintained that "fish don't bite as well during the dog days" of summer. Rogers reported that one African American fisherman, who never fished except when the wind was right, passed on a bit of advice:

> When de win's in de West
> De fishes bite de best;
> When de win's in the East
> De fishes bite de leas;
> De win' from de south
> Blows de bite in his mouf;
> De win' from the norf,
> De fish he don' come forth.

As with hunting, devotees of fishing developed special ways of increasing their yield. One such practice is called seining. The following account comes from North Carolina but probably reflected the custom among settlers in Wiregrass Country and elsewhere. "Seining in Panther Creek was ideal; it was not too wide for a twenty-foot seine to reach from bank to bank, at the lower end of a 'hole,' while three or four of us would jump in a hundred feet up and come down, each with a hoe, simply tearing up the creek bed. Just as we reached the lower end of the hole, the seine was raised, and sometimes two dozen fish were caught with one haul."

Another familiar method of fishing is known as "mudding." Ophelia White, an avid fish enthusiast, described one of her fondest memories:

> I know what we called back during that time, what we really called having a good time. . . . when there wasn't anything in the fields to do, then we would . . . , if it was hot, we would all get on the wagon; and we would ride through the woods. And it was what . . . what we called a creek. And I don't know whether you know what a creek is; but it's like a small river, just a small body of water, but its a long stream of it. And we would go and find places that . . . a lot of them was shallow and some of them were dried up in between.

Men using a net for pond fishing. Photo courtesy of Vanishing Georgia, Georgia Department of Archives and History, Atlanta.

And then you would find one that was deep enough to hold water, and it would have fish in it. And we would go what we would call mudding and we would walk out there and the water would come like up to our knees. And we would take a hoe and just go back and forth in there muddying the water, making the fish come up. It would make the fish drunk so that they would come up to the top. We could catch them. We loved doing that.

Some fishermen used natural ingredients to poison the fish. The following account appeared in Dave Stanley's field notes. "Mr. Rice mentioned fishing methods to me: a plant called devil's shoestring, which grows wild in the area, is an effective fish poison. The root is mashed up and dropped into a body of water; the poison makes the fish come to the surface. The same results can be obtained by taking black walnut hulls, still green, beating them up and putting them in the water. (—Griffin told me about poisons making the fish taste soft and flabby and that's why he doesn't use them)."

One fisherman remembered children using wiregrass to get bait. "[Chuck Royal] recalls using the stems of the wiregrass as a boy to get earthworms of the kind he called 'pink'—the same as night crawlers. You'd go to a swampy place and look for the worm holes in the ground, take a stem of wiregrass and push it down the hole and 'tickle' the worm. The worm would come out of the ground through another hole and could then be caught."

Wiregrass residents had several other ingenious ways of securing their bait. The practice of grunting worms, or worm fiddling, was prominent among them. Appropriately, "You use a staub and a brick, drive the staub in the ground, rub the brick back and forth to make the staub vibrate, worms came out the ground." At local festivals in Caryville, Florida, and Geneva, Alabama, worm fiddling has become a main attraction. Men, women, and children pair off in their respective divisions to see who can fiddle up the most worms.

Many women have developed a great passion for fishing and find ingenious ways to secure bait. Some have bait beds, which they irrigate with dishwater and enrich with household foods such as cornmeal. There is also a local bait industry, which hires workers to pack worms by the thousand for a nominal wage. Ophelia White spoke of the importance of fishing in her everyday life.

> I love fishing. At one time I was going everyday. For three or four weeks. . . .
> Then I had no one to go. Sometimes he [her oldest son] would call me. He
> would call back: "Ophelia, what are you doing today?" I'd say, "I don't know.
> Why?" He'd say, "you reckon we could catch anything if we went fishing."
> And I would say, "I don't know but I think it's worth a try." And we would
> just go fishing. It's really relaxing. If I don't catch anything, so. But if I just
> get a bite every thirty minutes even if I don't catch anything, it doesn't matter
> as long as something bites. We would play a game like big fishermen on T.V.
> If I got tense up about something, we would just go fishing. Once I got started
> I would say I got to go back tomorrow. When it gets real hot snakes get real
> bad and that not too good.

Most women in the Wiregrass have grown up believing that "woman's work is never done." Fishing may be an activity that simultaneously satisfies the work ethic while providing recreational pleasure.

Like the house, the yard is part of women's domain. Women not only design and tend gardens but also landscape and groom their yards. As scholar Mara Miller has observed, "Gardens are not only environments. They are also sites. By 'site' I mean a place designed and designated for a specific activity or purpose, as we speak of choosing a campsite or a site for a house or a new business." Yardscape designers arrange space with concern not only for aesthetic qualities but for the activities to be undertaken there. Their inner vision is realized incrementally. The project is always in process and never attains completion, for it represents a life's work.

Usually, a garden is the focal point of a yardscape. A porch and/or a sitting area, as well as a house, may complete the picture. Like the informal

Part of a yardscape by Katie Potts. Photo by Jerrilyn McGregory.

garden, yardscapes "are designed intuitively, in accordance with poetic or picturesque principles, or to imitate the natural landscape." In addition, gardens differ from yardscapes with regard to seating. Seating is usually tangential to a garden, whereas it is an intrinsic part of a yardscape.

The yardscape artists define themselves in the process of carrying out their work. Some approach the job as a form of problem solving, others as an extension of trade skills, and still others as self-imposed therapy. For instance, Katie Potts moved into a home with a yard that contained a dead cypress tree and a huge oak stump. She incorporated into the base of the dead tree a living floral arrangement with a trellis that allows a living vine to wind around it as it grows. The oak stump, painted white, now holds an array of flower pots along its stump and roots. Designers like Mrs. Potts often rely on container gardening for accents.

Gladys Westbrook is a retired African American schoolteacher. Born in Hazelcrest, Georgia, she spent most of her adult life teaching school and serving as first lady in her husband's church in Macon. When her husband changed pastorates, they came to Cairo, Georgia, where they lived together until his recent death. Mrs. Westbrook has designed a yardscape that uses children's toys to create an aura of enchantment. The resulting yardscape, which surreptitiously incorporates vegetables and fruits among the flowers, is a memorial both to her past occupation and to her long-term marriage.

Part of a yardscape by Gladys Westbrook, featuring children's toys. Photo by
Jerrilyn McGregory.

Mrs. Westbrook has planted two vines at opposite ends of a wire in the
shape of an M and a W, standing for Macon and her married name. Each
year the vines grow a little closer together.

Several yardscapes reflect their owners' needs to reconcile the present
with the past. African American Betty McDougal-Daffin cultivates a vege-
table and flower garden across from her home, where she puts into practice
the knowledge she acquired growing up in a farming community. Surrounding her house, she grows about a hundred exotic and domestic plants
largely acquired from a nursery where she worked.

McDougal-Daffin's commitments to her church, to her business, and to
a part-time job do not leave her enough time to tend all her plants, but her
yardscape has taken on a life of its own. Except for those plants that are
stored on her porch, many of the rest now flourish unassisted.

Katie Potts says that passers-by often ask her whether she is an artist.
She answers, "No, it just comes in my mind to do that." Most communities
have a yardscape artist or two. As Kathleen Condon has observed, "If these
builders are expressing anything in their work, it is simply their passion to
create."

At times, creators like Mrs. Poole (a white widow who asked to be identified by her surname alone) describe their yardscaping as therapy. Garden-

ing and work outdoors helps people heal from the loss of a mate, early retirement, and illness. According to Charles Lewis, "The power of gardens and landscapes to heal psychic stress arises from the personal equivalents of these gardens and landscapes in the mind of the viewer. Thus, for designers, the importance of their work lies more in the mental images they create than in the physical arrangement of plants and spaces."

Yardscapes thus fulfill both a personal and a communal function. The designers create in their mind's eye what they hope will be a positive visual experience for others. In so doing, the designers of healing spaces take responsibility for their own recovery and growth. In conversation they often manifest an inner beauty that matches the splendor of their creations.

Residents of Wiregrass Country today share experiences with roots deep in the historical past. This is not the "land that time forgot." It participates in and responds to the surrounding world, at the same time forming part of that world and remaining separate from it. Being mainly rural, it continues to be agricultural and also faces some of the conflicts associated with modern urban life.

People of different race, class, and culture interact in Wiregrass Country. They possess, as shown by the present volume, a sense of regional identity, of communal spirit. This cultural consciousness consists in part of a greater concern for the survival of others. Although house-raisings and logrollings are things of the past, most residents still feel the urge to participate in cooperative activities.

Wiregrass Country undeniably belongs to the Bible Belt. Apart from Christian fundamentalism, the label means that the people believe in collective work and collective responsibility. Many residents earn a living by manual labor. The industrial revolution, at least with respect to heavy manufacture, passed the Wiregrass region by. Longtime residents accustomed to working as wage earners came to depend on supplemental incomes—leasing land for hunting, selling marketable produce, or moonlighting during the harvest season. The work ethic typically remains strong.

Poverty and scarcity have led Wiregrass residents to be frugal in their habits. Their life histories describe hardships endured just to purchase the necessities of life. Those who own their land and homes are proud of the fact. The more affluent routinely share with the less affluent. Before there was an information superhighway, Wiregrass residents formed reciprocal support networks, and they continue to use these networks today.

In Wiregrass Country, residents' sense of place still derives from historic communities rather than from modern towns. People speak of living in Shiloh community, Friendship community, or Booker Hill. These locales, very close knit social environments, give their inhabitants a sense of belonging and identity.

Local residents take pride in their cultural inheritance. Today they compare their forebears' achievements favorably with those of people in other regions and see themselves as having benefited from their ancestors' habits of frugality and hard work. The past has left a legacy in tenacity and the ability to survive. While wiregrass itself no longer grows luxuriantly in the region, it has given people a resilience and an adaptability to change that augur well for the twenty-first century.

My special thanks go to the following people, who graciously provided interviews.

Harrison Bell, Cairo, Georgia, June 17, 1992
Jennifer Bland, Glennville, Georgia, May 27, 1994
Mary Blount, Tallahassee, Florida, June 7, 1994
Pearly Broome, Cairo, Georgia, June 7, 1994
Mandy Butler, Cairo, Georgia, June 9, 1994
E. W. Carswell, Chipley, Florida, May 6, 1994
Carolyn Chason, Cairo, Georgia, May 25, 1994
Dr. Wayne Faircloth, Valdosta, Georgia, June 16, 1994
Gail Fishman, Tallahassee, Florida, May 2, 1994
Henry Flores, Quincy, Florida, June 28, 1994
Tommie Gabriel, Thomasville, Georgia, March 23, 1994
Maria Garcia, Greensboro, Florida, May 19, 1994
Angus Gholson, Chattahootchee, Florida, May 19, 1994
Mary Louise Gilmore, Thomasville, Georgia, October 17, 1993
Jack Hadley, Thomasville, Georgia, May 25, 1994
Lizzie Henry, Tifton, Georgia, September 27, 1992
Japheth Jackson, Ozark, Alabama, July 15, 1992
John & Mary Jackson, Dothan, Alabama, November 27, 1992
Joy Jenks, Colquitt, Georgia, April 16, 1994
Willie & Louise Johnson, Thomasville, Georgia, January 15, 1994
Ralph Jones, Cairo, Georgia, June 6, 1994
Pokey Kirkland, Slocomb, Alabama, November 27, 1992
Doris Lewis, Dothan, Alabama, August 5, 1994
Luther Marable, Thomasville, Georgia, September 27, 1992
John McCullough, Pelham, Georgia, November 5, 1992
Betty McDougal-Daffin, Valdosta, Georgia, June 23, 1994
Boysie McGriff, Cairo, Georgia, July 13, 1992
Katie Nelson, Cairo, Georgia, July 18, 1992
David Null, Meigs, Georgia, December 10, 1992
Connie Palmer, Altha, Florida, August 31, 1994
Olin Pope, Barwick, Georgia, May 26, 1994

Carrine Porter, Bascom, Florida, November 28, 1992
Katie Potts, Troy, Alabama, September 28, 1992
James Richardson, Iron City, Georgia, June 29, 1994
Rev. Robinson, Cairo, Georgia, July 16, 1992
Wallace Sholar, Cairo, Georgia, May 17, 1994
Fred Smith, Cairo, Georgia, June 29, 1994
Stanley Smith, Ozark, Alabama, June 9, 1994
Tommy Spurlock, Ozark, Alabama, June 9, 1994
Gladys Westbrook, Cairo, Georgia, July 3, 1992
John Whitaker, Moultrie, Georgia, November 5, 1992
Ophelia White, Sylvester, Georgia, December 11, 1993
Dewey Williams, Ozark, Alabama, July 15, 1992
Agnes Windsor, Slocomb, Alabama, July 16, 1994
Bertha Wrice, Quitman, Georgia, May 27, 1994
Owen Wrice, Quitman, Georgia, June 16, 1994
Milton Young, Graceville, Florida, June 25, 1994

Introduction

Several works discuss plant life in the region, especially wiregrass. See Roland Harper, Florida Geological Survey, *Sixth Annual Report* (Tallahassee? 1914?); Richard M. Smith, *Wild Plants of America* (New York: John Wiley & Sons, 1989); Norman Christensen, "Vegetation of the Southeastern Coastal Plain," in *North American Terrestrial Vegetation*, ed. Michael Barbour and William Billings (Cambridge: Cambridge University Press, 1988), 317–63; Wayne Faircloth, "The Vascular Flora of Central South Georgia" (Ph.D. diss., University of Georgia, 1971); George Rogers and R. Frank Saunders, Jr., *Swamp Water and Wiregrass: Historical Sketches of Coastal Georgia* (Macon, GA: Mercer University Press, 1984); George Schwarz, *The Longleaf Pine in Virgin Forest* (New York: John Wiley & Sons, 1907); W. G. Wahlenberg, *Longleaf Pine* (Washington, DC: C. L. Pack Forestry Foundation, 1946); and Howard Weaver and David Anderson, *Manual of Southern Forestry* (Danville, IL: Interstate, 1954): 154–56. Two specialized articles investigate wiregrass in more detail: David Hall, "Is It Wiregrass?" *Natural Areas Journal* 9 (1989): 219–22, and Robert Peet, "A Taxonomic Study of *Aristida stricta* and *Aristida beyrichiana*," *Rhodora* 95 (1953): 25–37. Informant Tommie Gabriel in Thomasville, Georgia, on March 23, 1994, shared his personal knowledge about wiregrass ("You were asking"). Special thanks to the distinguished amateur botanist Angus Gholson, quoted here ("Knowing wiregrass"), whom I interviewed in Chattahoochee, Florida, on May 19, 1994, and to Gail Fishman of the Nature Conservancy, interviewed in Tallahassee, Florida, on May 2, 1994. Mary Tebo, "The Southern Piney Woods: Describers, Destroyers, Survivors" (M.A. thesis, Florida State University, 1985), and Mary Ellen Tripp, "Longleaf Pine Lumber Manufacturing in the Altamaha River Basin, 1865–1918" (Ph.D. diss., Florida State University, 1983), discuss the Wiregrass ecosystem.

Fire ecology is a generally misunderstood aspect of nature conservation. Some works that clarify the issues include: Roland Harper, "Historical Notes on the Relation of Fires to Forest," in *Proceedings, Tall Timbers Fire Ecology Conference*, Tallahassee, Florida, March 1–2, 1962, pp. 11–29; Edward Johnson, *Fire and Vegetation Dynamics* (New York: Cambridge University Press, 1992); E. V. Komarek, "The Use of Fire: An Historical Background," *Proceedings, Tall Timbers Conference*, 7–10; and Omer C. Stewart, "Burning and Natural Vegetation in the United States," *Geographical Review* 41 (1951): 317–20.

The use of fire by southern Indians is discussed in Edward Johnson, *Fire and Vegetation Dynamics*; Stewart, "Burning and Natural Vegetation," 319–20; Albert Crowdey, *This Land, This South: An Environmental History* (Lexington: University Press of Kentucky, 1983), 14. Also, Billy Joe Jackson of the Creek Nation in Okmulgee, Oklahoma, provided an interview, quoted here ("fire is everything"), in Albany, Georgia, on May 21, 1994. Uses of fire by settlers and their descendants are discussed in Thomas D. Clark, *The Greening of the South: The Recovery of Land and Forest*, (Lexington: University Press of Kentucky, 1984); H. L. Beadel, "Fire Impressions," *Proceedings, Tall Timbers Conference*, 1–6; Wahlenberg, *Longleaf Pine*, 57–67; Schwarz, *Longleaf Pine*, 47–87; Clifton Johnson, *Highways and Byways* (New York: Macmillan, 1918), 215; Douglas Helms, "Just Lookin' for a Home: The Cotton Boll Weevil and the South" (Ph.D. diss., Florida State University, 1977), 351–53; and H. L. Stoddard, "Use of Fire in Pine Forest and Game Lands of the Deep Southeast," *Proceedings, Tall Timbers Conference*, 30–42.

Psychologist John Shea's comments ("the light sound") appear in Stephen Pyne, "Our Pappies Burned the Woods: A Fire History of the South," in *Fire in America: Cultural History of Wildland and Rural Fire* (Princeton, NJ: Princeton University Press, 1982), 143–60. I quote Ed Komarek ("I have spent") from an epigraph in Robert Joseph Rubanowice, *A Sense of Place in Southern Georgia: Birdsong Plantation, Farm, and Nature Center* (Tallahassee, FL: South Georgia Historical Consortium, 1994), 208.

1. Origins

Wilbur Zelinsky, *The Cultural Geography of the United States* (Englewood Cliffs, NJ: Prentice-Hall, 1973), 123–25, was helpful regarding regional identity. Department of Agriculture, *Georgia Historical and Industrial* (Atlanta: George Harrison, 1901), 159–65, indicates the region's specific physiographic boundaries. See also Gregor Sebba, ed., *Georgia Studies: Selected Writings of Robert Preston Brooks* (Athens: University of Georgia Press, 1952), 112–17. Brooks designated the region's "white counties." The following works map the region in other ways: Charles Wharton, *The Natural Environments of Georgia* (Atlanta: Georgia Department of Natural Resources, 1978), and Joan Sears, *The First One Hundred Years of Town Planning in Georgia* (Atlanta: Cherokee, 1979). Kenneth Krakow, *Georgia Place-Names* (Macon, GA: Winship, 1975), also mentions the region. Frank Owsley's *Plain Folk of the Old South* (Baton Rouge: Louisiana State University Press, 1949), 154–62, which is considered a classic, mentioned several Wiregrass counties and differentiated them from the pine belt. Geologist

Roland Harper relies on specific physiography to map the "rolling wire-grass" in Georgia for a series of four articles in the *Georgia Historical Quarterly* and later published in monograph form by the author as *Development of Agriculture in Georgia from 1850–1920* (N.p.: University Press of Alabama, n.d).

Frank Owsley and certain revisionist historians have addressed the economic and social diversity of southern culture. For instance, see J. Wayne Flynt, *Poor but Proud: Alabama's Poor Whites* (Tuscaloosa: University of Alabama Press, 1989); Terry Jordan and Matti Kaups, *The American Backwoods Frontier* (Baltimore: John Hopkins University Press, 1989); and Grady McWhiney, *Cracker Culture: Celtic Ways in the Old South* (Tuscaloosa: University of Alabama Press, 1988). The local historian and journalist E. W. Carswell, in *Remembering Old Rhoady* (Tallahassee, FL: Rose, 1993), 66, and Ann Malone, "Piney Woods Farmers of South Georgia, 1850–1900: Jeffersonian Yeomen in an Age of Expanding Commercialism," *Agricultural History* 60 (1986): 52, also discuss the cracker stereotype.

Since no significant military action took place in Wiregrass Country, details about the war effort are scant; see Flynt, *Poor but Proud*, 36–39. Historian Allen Jones provides the best historical account about the region's ambiguous role, in "A Federal Raid into Southeast Alabama," *Alabama Review* 14 (1961): 259–68. Nonetheless, the various county histories play up their contributions.

See Roland Harper's statement about the Black Belt in a geographical report in *Economic Botany of Alabama* (N.p.: University Press of Alabama, June 1913), 90. The statement about the pine barrens was made by Robert Preston Brooks in *Georgia Studies*, 273. My discussion of subliminal identity in Wiregrass Country draws on Wilbur Zelinsky, *Cultural Geography*, 112. Malone, "Piney Woods Farmers," 52, discusses how an isolated environment affected Wiregrass culture. Frank Roebuck made editorial comments about the derogatory terms used to describe the region, in *Gleanings: A Community's Memories of People at the Crossroads of a Place*, ed. Wessie Connell et al. (Cairo, GA: Roddenberry Library, 1987), 286.

Offhand comments like Michael Bradshaw's in *Regions and Regionalism in the United States* (London: Macmillan Education, 1988), oversimplify the South. McWhiney, *Cracker Culture*, xv, properly notes that the oral culture has contributed to the scarcity of written records from this social class.

According to Ruth Hale's study, "A Map of Vernacular Regions in America" (Ph.D. diss., University of Minnesota, 1971), 90 percent of respondents in the Alabama Wiregrass knew the region by its vernacular name, giving the region the highest name recognition of any part of the state. Hale, however, located no informants in Florida or Georgia who did so, 76. On the Florida Wiregrass I have quoted E. W. Carswell, *Holmesteading* (Chipley, FL: author, 1986), 15.

I quote Harper ("loner and more") from Clifton Paisley, *The Red Hills of Florida, 1528–1865* (Tuscaloosa: University of Alabama Press, 1989), 7, which also supplied information about Tallahassee's land and vegetation. Walter Schwartz also discussed American Indian agriculture as it reduced wiregrass growth in Tallahassee, in "Conserving Forest Diversity in Northern Florida: From Landscapes to Populations" (Ph.D. diss., Florida State University, 1990), 24. In addition, cultural and economic development in Leon County, which had eighty-one planters, did not conform to that in Wiregrass counties. See Paisley, *The Red Hills*, appendixes 1, 2, and 3.

The paucity of writings about Wiregrass Country is particularly regrettable in view of the abundant material available on Appalachia. On the lack of scribes ("long histories of"), I quote Minnie Boyd, *Alabama in the Fifties* (New York: Columbia University Press, 1931), 12. In 1977, the American Folklife Center of the Library of Congress, at the request of Syd Blackmarr of the Arts Experiment Station in Tifton, Georgia, sent four professional folklorists, Tom Adler, Bill Lightfoot, Beverly Robinson, and Dave Stanley, to collect material on eight counties within the region. The resulting publication, *Sketches of South Georgia Folklife*, was edited by Carl Fleischauer and Howard Marshall, American Folklife Center, Library of Congress, Washington, D.C., 1977. In my own research, I worked primarily in a concentric circle radiating from Dothan, Alabama; I worked my way across toward Valdosta, going north to Tifton in Georgia, and then proceeding west to Troy and back south to Opp in Alabama and on through the Florida panhandle.

Dissertations proved quite useful sources of material for this book. Mariella G. Hartsfield, "A Collection and Study of the Traditional Prose Narrative in Grady County, Georgia" (Ph.D. diss., Florida State University, 1980), has been published in book form: *Tall Betsy and Dunce Baby: South Georgia Folktales* (Athens: University of Georgia Press, 1987).

J. L. Herring provided the most extensive descriptions of folk cultural traditions in the region, in *Saturday Night Sketches: Stories of Old Wiregrass Georgia* (Boston: Gorham, 1918). E. W. Carswell has produced more than fifteen books.

The following list of county histories is nearly complete: David Avant, Jr., *History of Gadsden County* (Tallahassee, FL: L'Avant Studios, 1985); Ruth Barron, *Footprints in Appling County* (Baxley, GA: Appling County Board of Commissioners, 1981); Bicentennial/Sesquicentennial Commission, *Heritage of Thomas County Georgia* (n.p., 1976); Dorothy Brannen, *Life in Old Bulloch: The Story of a Wiregrass County* (Gainesville, GA: Magnolia Press, 1987); Yvonne Brunton, *Grady County Georgia: Some of Its History,*

Folk Architecture, and Families (Jackson, MS: Quality Printers, 1979); E. W. Carswell, *Holmesteading* (Chipley, FL: author, 1986); and *Washington: Florida's Twelfth County* (Tallahassee, FL: Rose, 1991); J. B. Clements, *History of Irwin County* (n.p., 1932); James Dorsey, *Footprints Along the Hoopee: A History of Emanuel County, 1812–1900* (Gainesville, GA: Magnolia Press, 1989); James Dorsey and John Derden, *Montgomery County, Georgia: A Source Book of Genealogy and History* (Swainsboro, GA: Magnolia Press, 1983); M. P. Farmer, *One Hundred Fifty Years in Pike County, Alabama, 1821–1971* (Anniston, AL: Higginbotham, 1973); Geneva Woman's Club, *Geneva, Alabama: A History* (n.p., 1987); Georgia Griffin, *Ochlocknee: Land of Crooked Water* (Thomasville, GA: Ochlocknee Community Civic Club, 1982); Folks Huxford, *The History of Brooks County, Georgia* (Homersville, GA: author, 1949); Val McGee, *Claybank Memories: A History of Dale County, Alabama* (Ozark, AL: Dale County Historical Society, 1989); Floris Mann, *History of Telfair County from 1812 to 1949* (Spartanburg, SC: Reprint, 1978); M. O'Neal, *Prologue* (author, 1985); Paisley, *The Red Hills*; William Warren Rogers, *Thomas County, 1865–1900* (Tallahassee: Florida State University Press, 1973); J. T. Shelton, *Pines and Pioneers: A History of Lowndes County, Georgia, 1825–1900* (Atlanta: Cherokee, 1976); J. Randall Stanley, *History of Jackson County* (n.p.: Jackson County Historical Society, 1950); Wendell and Pamela Stepp, *Dothan: A Pictorial History* (n.p., 1984); Hoyt Warren, *Henry's Heritage* (Abbeville, AL: n.p., 1978); Fred Watson, *Coffee Grounds* (Anniston, AL: Higginbotham, 1970); Fred Watson, *Forgotten Trails* (Anniston, AL: Banner Books, 1968); Fred Watson, *Hub of the Wiregrass: A History of Houston County, Alabama, 1903–1972* (Anniston, AL: Higginbotham, 1972); Fred Watson, *Piney Wood Echoes* (Enterprise, AL: n.p., 1949); I. B. Williams, *History of Tift County* (Macon, GA: J. W. Burke, 1948); R. H. Wind, ed., *Grady, 1904–1953* (Cairo, GA: Messenger, 1983); and Miles Womack, Jr., *Gadsden: A Florida County in Word and Picture* (n.p., 1976).

2. Indians, Settlers, and Slaves

About the ancient inhabitants of Wiregrass Country, see Jesse Burt and Robert Ferguson, *Indians of the Southeast: Then and Now* (Nashville: Abingdon, 1973); Emma Lila Fundaburk and Mary Foreman, eds., *Sun Circles and Human Hands: The Southeastern Indians Art and Industries* (Montgomery, AL: Paragon Press, 1957); Clifton Paisley, *The Red Hills of Florida, 1528–1865* (Tuscaloosa: University of Alabama Press, 1989), 10–15; Ruth Murray Underhill, *Red Man's America* (Chicago: University of Chicago Press, 1953); John Walthall, *Prehistoric Indians of the Southeast: Archaeology of Alabama and the Middle South* (University: University of Alabama Press, 1980); Walter L. Williams, ed., "Southeastern Indians Before Removal: Prehistory, Contact, Decline," in *Southeastern Indians Since the Removal Era* (Athens: University of Georgia Press, 1979); and J. Leitch Wright, *The Only Land They Knew* (New York: Free Press, 1981).

Several comprehensive works present insights into the indigenous peoples exclusively in the Southeast: Burt and Ferguson, *Indians of the Southeast*; Fussell Chalker, *Pioneer Days Along the Ocmulgee* (Carrollton, GA: n.p., 1970); Robert Cotterill, *The Southern Indians: The Story of the Civilized Tribes Before Removal* (Norman: University of Oklahoma Press, 1954); Charles Hudson, ed., *Four Centuries of Southern Indians* (Athens: University of Georgia Press, 1975); Charles Hudson and Carmen Tesser, eds., *The Forgotten Centuries* (Athens: University of Georgia Press, 1994); Theda Perdue, *Nations Remembered: An Oral History of the Five Civilized Tribes, 1865–1907* (Westport, CT: Greenwood Press, 1980); John Swanton, *The Indians of the Southeastern United States* (1946; reprint, Washington, DC: Smithsonian, 1979); and Underhill, *Red Man's America*, 26–46.

Most regional texts begin with a focus on the Creek and/or Seminole Indians. Some of the more important include: James Covington, *The Seminoles of Florida* (Gainesville: University Press of Florida, 1993); James Doster, *Creek Indians and Their Florida Lands, 1740–1823*, Vols. 1 and 2 (New York: Garland, 1974); Charles Fairbanks, *Florida Indians III* (New York: Garland, 1974); Wayne Faircloth, "Just Their Names Persist: A Sketch of the Creek Indians and the South Georgia Frontier," in *Grady County Georgia: Some of Its History, Folk Architecture, and Families*, ed. Yvonne Brunton (Jackson, MS: Quality Printers, 1979), 8–21; Michael Green, *The Politics of Indian Removal* (Lincoln: University of Nebraska Press, 1982); Benjamin Griffith, Jr., *McIntosh and Weatherford, Creek Indian Leaders* (Tuscaloosa: University of Alabama Press, 1988); Harry Kersey, Jr., "Seminoles and Miccosukees: A Century in Retrospective," in *Indians of the Southeastern United States in the Late Twentieth Century*, ed. J. Anthony Paredes (Tuscaloosa: University of Alabama Press, 1992), 102–19; Paisley, *The Red Hills*, 44–104; William Winn, *The Old Beloved Path* (Eufaula, AL: Historic Chattahoochee Commission, 1992); William Sturtevant, ed., *A Creek Source Book* (New York: Garland, 1987); and J. Leitch Wright, *Creeks and Seminoles* (Lincoln: University of Nebraska Press, 1986) and *The Only Land They Knew*, 222–47. For a full etymology of "Seminole," see William Sturtevant, "Creek into Seminole," in *North American Indians in Historical Perspective*, ed. Eleanor Leacock and Nancy Lurie (New York: Random House, 1971).

Albert Gatschet, *A Migration Legend of the Creek Indians* (Philadelphia: Brinton, 1884), 180, discusses gender roles in effect during the celebration.

On other ethnological aspects, see John Hann, *Apalachee: The Land Between the Rivers* (Gainesville: University of Florida Press, 1988); Daniel Littlefield, *Africans and Creeks* (Westport, CT: Greenwood Press, 1977), 24–36. See also Peter Nabokov and Robert Easton, *Native American Architecture* (New York: Oxford University Press, 1989); Perdue, *Nations Remembered*; Underhill, *Red Man's America*, 26–46; Brent Weisman, *Like Beads on a String* (Tuscaloosa: University of Alabama Press, 1989); and Winn.

European exploration of the area is discussed in: Burt and Ferguson, *Indians of the Southeast*, 45–46; Hann, *Apalachee*; and Paisley, *The Red Hills*, 17–22. Spanish missions during this historic period and their effects on the aboriginal population are described in Bonnie McEwan, ed., *The Spanish Missions of La Florida* (Gainesville: University Press of Florida, 1993); Hann, *Apalachee*; and Paisley, *Red Hills*, 24–34. Moreover, Henry Dobyns, *Their Number Become Thinned* (Knoxville: University of Tennessee Press, 1983), delineates in detail the effect of European colonization on the American Indian population, especially the Timucuan-speaking group.

Many works touch upon trade's influence on the Creek Nation. See Hann, *Apalachee*, 148, and Williams, "Southeastern Indians," 16, on the subject of American trade practices. Also note Burt and Ferguson, *Indians of the Southeast*, 112–17, and Glorida Jahoda, *The Trail of Tears* (New York: Holt, Rinehart & Winston), 113–15, and Wright, *Creeks and Seminoles*. John Mahon, *History of the Second Seminole War, 1835–1842* (Gainesville: University of Florida Press, 1967), analyzes the complex issues that produced this war.

For treatment of the assimilation question, see Griffith, *McIntosh and Weatherford*. Michael Green, *Politics of Indian Removal*, analyzes in detail the social and political history of the Creeks leading to their removal. The African presence has also received full treatment. See William Willis, Jr., "Divide and Rule: Red, White, and Black in the Southeast," in *Red, White, and Black*, ed. Charles Hudson (Athens: Southern Anthropological Society, 1971), 99. Other texts that discuss the influential role played by Africans within indigenous groups are Fairbanks, *Florida Indians III*, William Loren Katz, *Black Indians* (New York: Atheneum, 1986); Harry Kersey, "The Cherokee, Creek, and Seminole Responses to Removal: A Comparison," in *Indians of the Lower South: Past and Present*, ed. John Mahon (Pensacola: Gulf Coast History and Humanities Conference, 1975), 112–17; George Klos, "Black Seminoles in Territorial Florida" (master's thesis, Florida State University, 1990); Littlefield, *Africans and Creeks*. See Wright, *Creeks and Seminoles*, 73–99, and, for the quotation of General Jesup ("a Negro not"), 275; and *The Only Land They Knew*, 248–78. Mahon, *History of the Second Seminole Wars*, furnished the information about the contributions of refugee Africans. Wright, in the chapter "Br-er Rabbit at the Square

Ground," in *The Only Land They Knew*, explains the amount of interracial social, political, and cultural interaction. See also Robert Anderson, "The End of an Idyll," *Florida Historical Quarterly* 42 (July 1963): 35–47. On Seminole slavery, see Russell Garvin, "The Free Negro in Florida Before the Civil War," *Florida Historical Quarterly* 46 (July 1967): 1–17.

For a fuller treatment of Indian Removal, see Williams, "Southeastern Indians," and, especially, Green, *Politics of Indian Removal*. Other relevant works include Burt and Ferguson, *Indians of the Southeast*, 173–90; Grant Foreman, *Indian Removal: The Emigration of the Five Civilized Tribes* (Norman: University of Oklahoma Press, 1952), relates the history of these American Indian groups after their removal to Oklahoma; Angie Debo, *A History of the Indians of the United States* (Norman: University of Oklahoma Press, 1970); and James Covington, *Seminoles*, 50–71. The county histories usually provide fairly comprehensive, although often biased, documentation of the settlement patterns of Wiregrass pioneers.

For tales of one runaway slave, see J. Russell Reaver, ed., *Florida Folktales* (Gainesville: University of Florida Press, 1987), 56–57. Carswell related yet another narrative (quoted here: "[The family]") during an interview in Chipley, Florida, on May 6, 1994. John Lovell, *Black Song* (New York: Paragon, 172), brings attention to a summation by W. E. B. Du Bois noting that runaways escaped along four geographical routes, including the swamps along the coast from Norfolk to North Florida, 173. Even after the Removal, fugitive slaves remained problematic for planters in the region. *Gleanings: A Community's Memories of People at the Crossroads of a Place*, ed. Wessie Connell et al. (Cairo, GA: Roddenberry Library, 1987), contains numerous nostalgic remarks endearing the homeplace ("The community is," 25). The statement about white man's country is quoted from Farmer, *One Hundred Fifty Years*, 18. For similar comments, see J. T. Shelton's *Pines and Pioneers*, 36–37, and other works.

3. Agriculture, Industry, and Labor

This chapter in part reflects research conducted during Jerry W. DeVine's association with the Wiregrass Georgia Rural History Project of the National Endowment for the Humanities and subsequent projects (1980–81, 1982–84). DeVine thanks Ann Patton Malone and Alberto Meloni, his colleagues in that project, and acknowledges his debt to the National Endowment for the Humanities and the Georgia Agrirama Development Authority, Tifton, Georgia, which sponsored the study.

The above-mentioned research projects amassed a significant collection of primary data mainly on social and economic aspects of the region's history between 1820 and 1920. The findings are summarized in several preliminary reports on various aspects of the inquiry and in final reports, all of which are archived with the research materials at Georgia Agrirama Development Authority, Tifton, Georgia. For the best overview of the subject, see Ann Patton Malone and Jerry W. DeVine, "Changes and Continuities in Wiregrass Georgia, 1870–1900" (Narrative Report for the National Endowment for the Humanities, Rural History Project, Washington, DC, 1981). Jerry W. DeVine, "Major Crops and Their Culture in Wiregrass Georgia, 1870–1900" (Tifton, GA: Rural History Project, Georgia Agrirama Development Authority, 1981), traces the transformation of the Wiregrass region's agriculture.

A comprehensive history of the Wiregrass region is yet to be published. Mark V. Wetherington's *The New South Comes to Wiregrass Georgia, 1860–1910* (Knoxville: University of Tennessee Press, 1994) is the first full-length study of the Georgia Wiregrass to appear in print, but it is limited to the postwar development of Georgia counties east of the Ocmulgee River. Somewhat broader treatments of the traditional society and of the economic development of the Georgia Wiregrass region appear in Ann Patton Malone, "Piney Woods Farmers of South Georgia, 1850–1900: Jeffersonian Yeomen in an Age of Expanding Commercialism," *Agricultural History* 60 (Fall 1986): 51–72, and Jerry W. DeVine, "Town Development in Wiregrass Georgia," *Journal of Southwest Georgia History* 1 (Fall 1983), 1–22.

The Wiregrass region is mentioned in many secondary studies, but the geographical definition of the region varies from work to work. Accurate, although differing, definitions of the Georgia Wiregrass are found in Robert Preston Brooks, *The Agrarian Revolution in Georgia, 1865–1912* (1914; reprint, Westport, CT: Greenwood, 1970), and Roland M. Harper, "Development of Agriculture in Lower Georgia from 1850 to 1880," *Georgia Historical Quarterly* 6 (1922): 97–121. The geographical definition of the region in Alabama that appears in Marie Bankhead Owen, LL.D., *The Story of Alabama: A History of the State*, 5 vols. (New York: Lewis Historical Publishing, 1949), 1:8–9, excludes the counties of Barbour, Crenshaw, Dale, and Pike, which were affected by the antebellum spread of cotton culture. Portions of these counties should be included with modern Coffee, Covington, Geneva, Henry, and Houston Counties in a description of the historical region. The historical Wiregrass region extends to the Florida panhandle counties of Bay, Calhoun, Gadsden, Holmes, Jackson, Liberty, Okaloosa, Walton, and Washington. With the exception of Holmes County, these counties also contain coastal and tidal river areas that are geographically and historically distinct. Jackson and Gadsden Counties, for instance, may be considered historically part of the Florida Black Belt. Except in the period census reports and state agricultural publications, the region is not generally identified in Florida histories.

Accounts of the Wiregrass region's economic history are scattered through many secondary works, the most informative being those concerning agriculture. Although the region is not specifically examined in Lewis Cecil Gray, *History of Agriculture in the Southern States to 1860*, 2 vols. (1941; reprint, Gloucester, MA: Peter Smith, 1958), this monumental study is an important source on agricultural development in and around the region. James C. Bonner's *History of Georgia Agriculture, 1732–1860* (Athens: University of Georgia Press, 1964), a basic source, includes the observation: "This region's agricultural development also does not articulate with the story of Georgia's expanding cotton industry in the period before 1860" (43). Willard Range, in *A Century of Georgia Agriculture, 1850–1950* (1954; reprint, Athens, GA: University of Georgia Press, 1969), does not distinguish the Wiregrass region from "South Georgia" in his analysis of agricultural development after 1865. Steven Hahn, *The Roots of Southern Populism: Yeoman Farmers and the Transformation of the Georgia Upcountry, 1850–1890* (New York: Oxford University Press, 1983), 144–52, deals with the economic and social transition in the Georgia upcountry (upper piedmont) during the same period and has some insights into developments in the Wiregrass region. Other useful sources on the Georgia Wiregrass include: Samuel G. McLendon, *History of the Public Domain of Georgia* (Atlanta, GA: Foote and Davies, 1924); James E. Callaway, *The Early Settlement of Georgia* (Athens: University of Georgia Press, 1948); Walter Zelinsky, "An Isochronic Map of Georgia Settlement, 1750–1850," *Georgia Historical Quarterly* 35 (1951): 191–95; Kenneth Coleman, ed., *A History of Georgia* (Athens: University of Georgia Press, 1977). W. T. Cash, *The Story of Florida*, 4 vols. (New York: American History Society, 1938), contains both a general overview of agricultural development in the state and brief articles on the economic history of the various counties.

The dynamics of antebellum economic development in the Southeast and the commercial isolation of the Wiregrass region are elaborated in the following studies: Ulrich B. Phillips, "The Origin and Growth of the Southern Black Belts," *American Historical Review* 11 (July 1906): 798–817; James C. Bonner, "Advancing Trends in Southern Agriculture, 1840–1860," *Agricultural History* 22 (October 1948): 248–59; Gavin Wright, "Economic Democracy and the Concentration of Agricultural Wealth in the Cotton South, 1850–1860," *Agricultural History* 44 (January 1970): 63–94; James D. Foust, "The Yeoman Farmer and Westward Expansion of U.S. Cotton Production" (Ph.D. diss., University of North Carolina, Chapel Hill, 1968); Robert L. De Coin, *History and Cultivation of Cotton and Tobacco* (Wilmington, Del., 1973).

The economic impact of the Civil War is discussed in Peter Wallenstein, "Rich Man's War, Rich Man's Fight: Civil War and the Transformation of Public Finance in Georgia," *Journal of Southern History* 50 (February 1984): 15–39; T. Conn Bryan, *Confederate Georgia* (Athens: University of Georgia Press, 1953); Robert Preston Brooks, "Conscription in the Confederate States of America, 1861–1865," *Military Historian and Economist* 1 (October 1916): 419–42.

Some relevant sources on railroad development include: Ulrich B. Phillips, *A History of Transportation in the Eastern Cotton Belt* (New York: Columbia University Press, 1908); Peter S. McGuire, "The Railroads of Georgia, 1860–1880," *Georgia Historical Quarterly* 16 (1932): 179–93.

Literature on the impoverishment of the rural South after the Civil War, in the fields of economics and social science as well as history, is extremely rich. Various approaches to this subject are represented by: Harold D. Woodman, "Post Civil War Southern Agriculture and the Law," *Agricultural History* 53 (January 1979): 319–37; Enoch Banks, *The Economics of Land Tenure in Georgia* (New York, 1905); Gilbert C. Fite, "The Agricultural Trap in the South," *Agricultural History* 60 (Fall 1986): 39–50; David L. Cohn, *The Life and Times of King Cotton* (New York, 1956); Gavin Wright and Howard Kunreuther, "Cotton, Corn, and Risk in the Nineteenth Century," *Journal of Economic History* 35 (September 1975): 526–28; J. Wayne Flynt, "Spindle, Mine, and Mule: The Poor White Experience in Post-Civil War Alabama," *Alabama Review* 34 (1981): 244–46; J. Crawford King, "The Closing of the Southern Range: An Exploratory Study," *Journal of Southern History* 48 (1982): 53–70.

Articles dealing with politics and the agrarian revolt are: William Warren Rogers, Jr., "Alabama and the Presidential Election of 1836," *Alabama Review* 35 (April 1982): 111–14; Judson K. Ward, "The New Departure Democrats of Georgia: An Interpretation," *Georgia Historical Quarterly* 41 (September 1957): 227–36; James O. Knauss, "The Farmers' Alliance in Florida," *South Atlantic Quarterly* 25 (July 1926): 300–15. William F. Holmes, "Moonshiners and Whitecaps in Alabama, 1893," *Alabama Review* 34 (January 1981): 31–49. Although this article does not deal with "whitecapping" in the Wiregrass region, the narrative and notes provide an explanation of the term and the background of events that also occurred in the region.

The chief source for statistical analysis of the population of the Wiregrass region from 1820 to 1920 is the manuscript federal census. The population or household schedules, grouped by state and period county, provide demographic data for statistical sampling from every census period except 1890 (most of the original manuscripts were destroyed in a fire). The agricultural schedules are available for the 1840 through 1880 census periods, as is an industrial schedule. These sources allow the researcher to evaluate and compare agricultural and commercial development in different localities.

The official compilation of each census is published in a multivolume set of reports. The reports of particular interest to this study are: U.S. Ninth Census (1870), *Reports*, vol. 3, *The Statistics of the Wealth and Industry of the United States* (Washington, DC, 1872); U.S. Tenth Census (1880), *Reports*, vol. 3, *Report of the Productions of Agriculture* (Washington, DC, 1883); U.S. Tenth Census (1880), *Reports*, vol. 6, *Cotton Production in the United States* (Washington, DC, 1881); U.S. Eleventh Census (1890), *Reports*, vol. 3, *Report on the Statistics of Agriculture in the United States* (Washington, DC, 1895); Twelfth Census (1900), *Reports*, vol. 5, *Agriculture, Part 1: Farms, Livestock, and Animals* (Washington, DC, 1902); U.S. Twelfth Census (1900), *Reports*, vol. 6, *Agriculture, Part 2: Crops and Irrigation* (Washington, DC, 1902).

The records and period publications of local, state, and federal governments are very valuable sources: See State of Georgia, Public Service Commission, "Annual Reports of Railroads . . . to the Railroad Commission, Savannah, Florida and Western Railroad, 1894," and "Annual Reports of Railroads . . . to the Railroad Commission, Brunswick and Western Railroad, 1894" (Atlanta: Georgia Department of Archives and History, 1894); Georgia State Department of Agriculture, *Publications*, 32 vols. (Atlanta, 1875–1904); U.S. Department of Agriculture, *Farmers' Bulletins Nos. 101– 125* (Washington, DC, 1899); U.S. Department of Agriculture, *Report of the Commissioner of Agriculture for the Year 1866* (Washington, DC, 1867); U.S. Department of Agriculture, *Report of the Commissioner of Agriculture for the Year 1883* (Washington, DC, 1883).

Although often inaccurate and partisan, newspaper accounts provide research leads and information not available in other sources. Newspapers surveyed include, for Alabama: *Abbeville Times*, 7 July 1896; *Covington Times* (Andalusia), 6, 20 March 1896; *Our Country and Its Future* (Cottondale), 1899; *Wiregrass Siftings* (Dothan), 1895–96; *Eufaula Times and News*, 1889–92, 1895–96; *Geneva Record*, 8 April, 10 June 1891; *Headland Sun*, 1896; *Montgomery Advertiser*, 1874–79, 1898–1902; *Troy Messenger*, 1896. For Florida: *Pensacola Daily News*, 1895–96; *Weekly Floridian* (Tallahassee), 1874–78, 1888–1892. For Georgia: *Albany Herald*, 1886–1905; *Berrien County Pioneer* (Sparks), 1888–1892; *Blackshear Times*, 24 October 1889; *Douglas Breeze*, 1895–96, 1899; *Fitzgerald Colony Citizen*, 31 December 1896; *People's Party Paper* (Atlanta), 1891–93; *Tifton Gazette*, 1892–1912; *Valdosta Times*, 1876–78, 1888–97.

Other primary sources included: T. B. Thorpe, "Sea Island Cotton," *Frank Leslie's Illustrated Newspaper*, 17 April 1869; *The Georgia Land and*

Lumber Company, Organized June 3, 1868 (New York, 1870); Richard Keily, *A Brief Descriptive and Statistical Sketch of Georgia* . . . (London, 1849); Governor William J. Northen Papers, Georgia State Department of Archives and History, Atlanta; J. L. Herring, *Saturday Night Sketches: Stories of Old Wiregrass Georgia* (1918; reprint: Tifton, GA: Sunny South Press, 1978).

The quotes appear in the following sources: *Tifton Gazette* ("The pork and"), 21 December 1894; Richard Keily, *A Brief Descriptive and Statistical Sketch of Georgia* . . . (London: J. Carroll, 1849), 25–26 ("They say little").

Wiregrass Country's soil got a bad press. On its poor quality see Ann Patton Malone, "Piney Woods Farmers," 52. For the text of Henry Grady's diversification speech, see *New South: Writings and Speeches of Henry W. Grady* (Savannah: Beehive Press, 1971). Mariella Hartsfield discusses diversification in the context of the Georgia Wiregrass in *Tall Betsy and Dunce Baby: South Georgia Folktales* (Athens: University of Georgia Press, 1987), 21–22. Kathryn Braund discusses the Alabama side of the equation in " 'Hog Wild' and 'Nuts': Billy Boll Weevil Comes to the Alabama Wiregrass," *Agricultural History* 63 (1989): 15–39. On the diversified South, see also Gilbert Fite, *Cotton Fields No More: Southern Agriculture, 1865–1980* (Lexington: University of Kentucky, 1984), 68–90.

Agnes Windsor, interviewed in Slocomb, Alabama, on July 16, 1994, supplied the prototypical example pertaining to African American immigration ("Alex Johnson was"). For a fictionalized account by a noted African American writer, see Margaret Walker, *Jubilee* (New York: Bantam Books, 1966), which describes much of the ordeal faced by African Americans new to the region. In addition, see Walker's *How I Wrote "Jubilee"* on the research behind this historical novel. On the relative affluence of the African American Wiregrass farmer, see Roland Harper, *Development of Agriculture in Georgia from 1850 to 1920*, reprinted from four articles in the *Georgia Historical Quarterly* (University, AL: author, n.d.), 335. For accounts of the other African American Wiregrass towns, see Fred Watson, *Piney Woods Echoes* (Enterprise, AL: n.p., 1949), 118.

Gleanings: A Community's Memories of People at the Crossroads of a Place, ed. Wessie Connell et al. (Cairo, GA: Roddenberry Library, 1987), amounts to a genealogical reference source based on reminiscences and family histories contributed by numerous members of Grady County, Georgia. I quote statements about the exodus of families into diversified Georgia from Lorena Matilda Huett Brinson ("A group was sent") and Jewell Reagan Walker ("rich and fertile"), respectively, 123 and 208.

About the economic system based on tolls and barter, see Georgia Griffin's *Ochlocknee: Land of Crooked Waters* (Thomasville, GA: Ochlocknee Community Civic Club, 1982), 13 (quotation: "People went to"). J. Wayne Flynt, *Poor but Proud*, also helpfully illuminates the system of barter and trade, 10. In an interview on June 6, 1994, Pearly Broome of Cairo, Georgia, spoke of her own experience with the practice ("we put up"). On the lack of genuine poverty, I quote Malone, "Piney Woods Farmers," 52 ("more free of").

The Wiregrass cowman, under various names, has been the focus of several studies. Malone, "Piney Woods Farmers," prefers the term "wiregrass ranger," 61. See also Joe Akerman, Jr., *Florida Cowman: A History of Florida Cattle Raising* (Kissimmee, FL: Florida Cattlemen's Association, 1966). Most works on the subject note in passing that although central Florida became a sort of capital for cowmen, they were the descendants of Wiregrass pioneers. See also E. W. Carswell, *Holmesteading* (Chipley, FL: author, 1986), 150–53; H. L. Stoddard, "Uses of Fire in Pine Forests and Game Lands of the Southeast," *Proceedings, Tall Timbers Conference*, 35–37, emphasizes the importance of the cattlemen in the area. Frank Owsley was among the first to recognize two classes of herdsmen in *Plain Folk of the Old South* (Baton Rouge: Louisiana State University Press, 1949), 24–45. Also, the farmer Olin Pope supplied primary documentation in an interview in Barwick, Georgia, on May 26, 1994 ("They had [an African American]"). About ranging practices I have quoted John Solomon Otto, "Traditional Cattle-Herding Practices," *Journal of American Folklore* 97 (1984): 299, and *The Southern Frontiers, 1607–1860* (Westport, CT: Greenwood Press, 1989), 114–15. Many county histories mention the practice in passing; see, for instance, Dorothy Brannen, *Life in Old Bulloch County, Georgia* (n.p., 1976), 90. For a relatively comprehensive account of the fence law controversy in Georgia, see Charles Flynn, Jr., *White Land, Black Labor: Caste and Class in Late Nineteenth-Century Georgia* (Baton Rouge: Louisiana State University Press, 1983), 128–36.

Francis Simkins commented on "The South" as a historic region of the United States in *Regionalism in America*, ed. Merrill Jensen (Madison: University of Wisconsin Press, 1951), 167. For more details regarding shade tobacco, see David Avant, Jr., *History of Gadsden County* (Tallahassee, FL: L'Avant Studios, 1985), 151–73. The introduction of flue tobacco by the Burroughs clan is discussed in Connell, ed., *Gleanings*, 123. I obtained other valuable information from an interview with Carolyn Chason, a local historian in Cairo, Georgia, on May 25, 1994 ("It filtered the").

Wiregrass Country's march toward progress is discussed in James Mc-Corkle, "Moving Perishables to Market: Southern Railroads and the Nineteenth-Century Origins of Southern Truck Farming," *Agricultural History* 66 (1992): 71. Peanuts became synonymous with diversification. I see Douglas Helms, "Just Lookin' for a Home: The Cotton Boll Weevil and the South" (Ph.D. diss., Florida State University, 1977). Many of the county histories describe the role played by the peanut in the economic and social life of their locale. Fite in *Cotton Fields* supplied fuller details about its production and problems. Carswell mentioned the initiation of pecans to the region in *Holmesteading*, 170–71.

Hartsfield furnished the quoted statement about how workers diversified in order to maintain their farms as a way of life ("worked for about"), 42. Most county histories mention the status of turpentining and lumbering in their locales, but Brannen supplied most of the details, including those about the impact of African American outmigration in pursuit of these industries, 73–80. Also, the local history researched and compiled by Ruth Barron, *Footprints in Appling County* (Baxley, GA: Appling County, 1981), includes a thorough treatment of naval stores and the timber industry in that section. On nostalgic recollections of turpentining, see Clifton Johnson, *Highways and Byways* (New York: Macmillan, 1918), 214–16 ("Often you hear"); Carswell, *Holmesteading*, 146–49 ("By listening"). For additional information about African Americans and lumbering, see Flynt, *Poor but Proud*. Several interviews supplied oral histories to match the written literature: Dr. Wayne Faircloth was interviewed in Valdosta, Georgia, on June 16, 1994, and I also interviewed Owen Wrice, a retired African American railroad worker, in Quitman, Georgia (quotation: "Every individual out"). For particulars about lumbering and men who lived on the rails, see Mary Tebo, "The Southern Piney Woods" (M.A. thesis, Florida State University, 1985), 18–29. Also, Mary Tripp treats the lumber industry extensively in her "LongLeaf Pine Lumber Manufacturing" (Ph.D. diss., Florida State University, 1983).

Malone discussed the relative loss of autonomy of workers as landowners in Wiregrass Georgia; see "Piney Woods Farmers," 79. On the demise of King Cotton as a symbol—the most obvious difference that diversification brought to Wiregrass Country—see Braund, " 'Hog Wild,' " 39. I have quoted Brinson ("I worked at") from Connell, ed., *Gleanings*, 19. I quote the statement about stable communal life ("People say, 'come' ") from Mary Ann Powell, *Five Communities* (Athens: University of Georgia, 1991), 317. During an interview, Tommie Gabriel eagerly detailed his community sharing ("If a man").

The "new immigrant" experience in Wiregrass Country gains substance from the *1992 County and City Data Book*, ed. Curtenay Slater and George Hall (Lanham, MD: Bernan, 1992). Wilbur Zelinsky in *The Cultural Geography of the United States* (Englewood Cliffs, NJ: Prentice-Hall, 1973), states that outside some particularly large urban centers of the South, immigrant communities were relatively rare. In addition, Raymond Gastil, *Cultural Regions of the United States* (Seattle: University of Washington Press, 1975), discussed immigrants' concern about freedom in the South, 181.

Not surprisingly, there is little documentation of the Jewish American presence in the Wiregrass. A modest pamphlet, *Thomasville Jewish Community History*, by Herman Rosenberg (n.p., n.d), may be the only publication in this area. For a monograph treating Jewish immigrants in the South in general, see Mark Elovitz, *A Century of Jewish Life in Dixie: The Birmingham Experience* (University: University of Alabama Press, 1974). William Rogers, *Thomas County, 1865–1900* (Tallahassee: Florida State University Press, 1973), discussed a fundamental lack of anti-Semitism and how Jewish merchants became accepted leaders of town life in Thomasville, 176. The announcement appeared in the *Cairo Messenger*, October 22, 1906.

For works dealing with contemporary American Indian populations in Wiregrass Country, see J. Anthony Paredes, "Back from Disappearance: The Alabama Creek Indian Community," in *Southeastern Indians Since the Removal Era*, ed. Walter Williams (Athens: University of Georgia Press, 1979), 123–41; "The Folk Culture of the Eastern Creek Indians: Synthesis and Change," in *Indians of the Lower South: Past and Present*, ed. John Mahon (Pensacola: Gulf Coast History and Humanities Conference, 1975); and "The Emergence of Contemporary Eastern Creek Identity," in *A Creek Source Book*, ed. William Sturdevant (New York: Garland, 1987). For an ethnographic description of the annual busk, see Albert Gatschak, *A Migration Legend of the Creek Indians* (Philadelphia: Brinton, 1884), 177–83; James Buswell, "Florida Seminole Religious Ritual: Resistance and Change" (Ph.D. diss. Saint Louis University, 1972); and George Klos, "Black Seminoles in Territorial Florida" (M.A. thesis, Florida State University, 1990).

As part of his petition to achieve recognition, Andrew Ramsey had printed *Florida Tribe of Eastern Creek Indians* (Bruce, FL: Florida Tribe of Eastern Creek Indians, 1978). The statements that I have quoted about the dispersal of American Indians and strategies by which their families survived appear on pages 117 and 47–48, respectively.

4. Rafthands of the Altamaha River

While scholars have described timber workers of the eastern and northwestern United States, the rafthands who made possible the great timber industry in Georgia have gone unnoticed. A regional study of folklore that reflects the cultural background of rafthands is volume 7 of the Frank C. Brown Collection of North Carolina Folklore, edited by Wayland D. Hand, *Popular Beliefs and Superstitions from North Carolina* (Durham: Duke University Press, 1964). Some of the Altamaha rafthands' occupational lore compares with that described in Roland Palmer Gray's *Songs and Ballads of the Maine Lumberjacks* (Cambridge, MA: Harvard University Press, 1925);

Franz Rickaby's *Ballads and Songs of the Shanty-Boy* (Cambridge, MA: Harvard University Press, 1926); Earl Clifton Beck's *Songs of the Michigan Lumberjacks* (Ann Arbor: University of Michigan Press, 1941). The rich traditions of Canada appear in Edith Fowke's *Lumbering Songs from the Northern Woods* (Austin: American Folklore Society and the University of Texas Press, 1970). Robert Tristram Coffin's *Kennebec* (New York: Houghton Mifflin, 1937) deals with the folklore and folkways of the people of Maine's fabled river.

Three novelists who have incorporated the life and lore of the Altamaha rafthands into their work are Kirk Munroe, Caroline Miller, and Brainard Cheney. Munroe wrote fiction for young readers in the 1890s, and his thorough familiarity with the life of the rafthand is evident in *Shine Terrill, A Sea-Island Ranger* (Boston: Lothrop Publishing, 1899) ("Fried catfish"; "Finally a black"). Caroline Miller's novel *Lamb in His Bosom* (New York: Houghton Mifflin, 1935), which won the Pulitzer Prize, has cameos of rafthands, including women who accompanied their husbands.

The most extensive fictional treatment of the rafthand appears in the novels of Brainard Cheney (quotation: "Rope around my"), a native of Lumber City who served as a rafthand before he attended Vanderbilt University. There he learned to love literature and, encouraged by his roommate Robert Penn Warren, he began writing novels of his own. All four of his novels are set in the Altamaha river valley: *Lightwood* (New York: Houghton Mifflin, 1939); *River Rogue* (New York: Houghton Mifflin, 1942); *This Is Adam* (New York: McDowell, Oblensky, 1958); *Devil's Elbow* (New York: Crown Publishing, 1969). *River Rogue* treats the folklore of the Altamaha region. *This Is Adam* describes the racial interaction that a character experiences in early childhood.

Lydia Parrish transcribed songs from the timber docks of Darien and St. Simons Islands in *Slave Songs of the Georgia Sea Islands* (New York: Creative Age Press, 1942). James Cook and Andrew Buckley of McIntosh County were especially good sources of music from the Darien docks. Bessie Lewis, the local historian of McIntosh County, collected some of their music and anecdotes. Upon her death in 1983, Miss Lewis's papers were placed in the collections of the Georgia Historical Society in Savannah. Mr. Cook shared "Soldier of the Cross" and his interpretation of it with the author on August 26, 1973 ("gave them the").

Author Delma E. Presley thanks a number of former rafthands and timber workers who provided interviews: Perry Collins, Twin City, Georgia, March 1972; James Kelton Rollison ("would have bad"), Hilton Head, South Carolina, December 1972 and July 1983; Jessie Yeomans, Brunswick, Georgia, July 1973 "A woman waded"); Green Deen, Baxley, Georgia, November 1981; Bill Deen, Deen's Landing, Georgia, January–April 1982 ("depends on where"); Holland Madray, Madray Springs, Georgia, January–April 1982; Claude Stewart, Hazlehurst, Georgia, February–March 1982; Curtis Ryalls, Darien, Georgia, August 1981–April 1982; Elijah Barwick, McIntosh County, Georgia, January 1982; Henry Eason, Surrency, Georgia, April 1982. Colleagues at Georgia Southern University have assisted and sometimes accompanied the author in interviews and research projects. Presley's grateful for their help: George A. Rogers, R. Frank Saunders, Lewis Selvidge, Hugh Darley, Gordon O'Neal, John Eaton, Sue Smith, and Alan Kaye. Finally, Delma E. Presley quotes a fellow rafter ("What the hell").

5. The Sacred Harp and Southern Gospel Music

Unlike other southern regions, Wiregrass Country has seen no published research into its musical traditions apart from the Sacred Harp tradition. William Lynwood Montell, however, the editor of the Folklife in the South series, has recently published *Singing the Glory Down: Amateur Gospel Music in South Central Kentucky, 1900–1990* (Lexington: University Press of Kentucky, 1991), which I found extremely helpful. Although it documents southern gospel music in central Kentucky, much of its information applies to Wiregrass Country today.

This chapter discusses regional music mainly in light of ethnography and oral histories. Olin Pope, a white farmer, expressed his preference for sacred music in an interview in Barwick, Georgia, on May 26, 1994. The musicologist Lois Blackwell, in *The Wings of the Dove: The Story of Gospel Music in America* (Norfolk, VA: Donning, 1978), provides a history of the popular singers within the southern gospel musical tradition. Bill Malone's *Southern Music/American Music* (Lexington: University Press of Kentucky, 1979) touches on several key points relating to gospel in the southern tradition. Don Cusic in *The Sound of Light: A History of Gospel Music* (Bowling Green, OH: Bowling Green State University Popular Press, 1990) defines southern gospel music mainly as the subgenre that's country gospel music in my text.

Several works document camp meetings and revivals in nineteenth-century America. Dickson Bruce in *And They All Sang Hallelujah: Plain-Folk Camp-Meeting Religion, 1800–1845* (Knoxville: University of Tennessee Press, 1974) has reported that camp meetings virtually disappeared by 1840. County histories from the Wiregrass, however, consistently report that camp meetings continued uninterrupted into the twentieth century. Sandra Sizer in *Gospel Hymns and Social Religion* (Philadelphia: Temple University, 1978) theorizes about the use of language and culture in relation to revivalism in the urban North. Dorothy Horn compares *The Southern Harmony* and *The Original Sacred Harp* and *The New Harp of Columbia* with a very technical analysis.

Sacred Harp music draws upon American secular songs as well as upon revival spirituals. See Dorothy Horn, *Sing to Me of Heaven: A Study of Folk and Early American Materials in Three Old Harp Books* (Gainesville: University of Florida Press, 1970), 38; Buell Cobb, *The Sacred Harp: A Tradition and Its Music* (Athens: University of Georgia Press, 1978), 30–32. Cobb also discusses the role of different revisions on singing communities, 82–117. Daniel Patterson's remarks are quoted from Dave Stanley's article "The Gospel-Singing Convention in South Georgia," *Journal of American Folklore* 95 (1982): 7. Hugh McGraw's quoted statement ("It's a dying") appeared in Richard DeLong, "Fasola Singing: Its History and Traditions," *National Sacred Harp Newsletter*, February 1989, p. 5. Several newsletters came into existence to support the musical tradition. The *National Sacred Harp Newsletter* is now defunct. Karen Luke Jackson, "The Royal Singing Convention, 1793–1931," *Georgia Historical Quarterly* 56 (1972): 495–509, furnishes further documentation.

Dave Stanley, "The Gospel-Singing Convention," significantly updated information pertaining to the seven-shape note singing conventions in south central Georgia when they had almost ceased and supplied the quoted comment ("Back then, say") about their social function, 13. Karen Jackson, "The Royal Singing Convention," 500, supplied the information about excursion trains to the sites. Edith Card presents a history of the tradition and the shift to seven notes in "The Tradition of Shaped-Note Music," in *Foxfire* 7 (Garden City, NY: Anchor, 1982), 280–95. On the tradition's utility and meaning for participants, see the letter to the editor, *National Sacred Harp Newsletter*, January 1990, p. 5 ("At a singing").

Cobb, *Sacred Harp*, 19–20, treats the Primitive Baptist connection as implicit in the shape note tradition. Cobb has indicated that the same texts were generally used, although the Primitive Baptists rely on the *Old School Hymnal*, Cayce's *Good Old Songs*, and Lloyd's *Hymns*. Ralph Stanley, a Primitive Baptist bluegrass performer, supplied the statement ("Well, that's the") about his personal experience within his church in an interview with Howard Marshall, " 'Keep on the Sunny Side of Life': Pattern and Religious Expression in Bluegrass Gospel Music," *New York Folklore Quarterly* 30 (1974): 21. The observations regarding the Church of Christ reflect interviews with members following ethnographic contact with the Washington Street Church of Christ in Quincy, Florida.

The quotation of Japheth Jackson gives the context for the compilation of *The Colored Sacred Harp*. For a definitive history of the Sacred Harp, see Cobb, *The Sacred Harp*. Joe Dan Boyd has written an excellent biography of Judge Jackson, the author of *The Colored Sacred Harp*, "Judge Jackson: Black Giant of White Spirituals," *Journal of American Folklore* 83 (October–December, 1970): 446–51. Southeast Alabama's African American Sacred Harp singing community is the subject of an extensive musicological analysis in Doris Dyen's "The Role of Shape-Note Singing in the Musical Culture of Black Communities in Southeast Alabama" (Ph.D. diss., University of Illinois at Urbana-Champaign, 1977). The several recordings of African American Sacred Harp singing that are commercially available include: Kathryn King, producer, *The Colored Sacred Harp: Wiregrass Sacred Harp Singers*, New World Records, New York, 1993; and Henry Willett, producer, *Wiregrass Notes: Black Sacred Harp Singing from Southeast Alabama*, Alabama Traditions, Montgomery, AL, 1982.

In 1938, Fisk University's John Work was the first to turn scholarly attention to Alabama's African American Sacred Harp community. Work heightened awareness of the tradition when he traveled to Ozark and recorded four discs that are now deposited at the Library of Congress. He also carried back a number of copies of *The Colored Sacred Harp*. Music scholar George Pullen Jackson subsequently became acquainted with *The Colored Sacred Harp* and mentioned it in both *White and Negro Spirituals* and *The Story of the Sacred Harp*. In both cases, he largely dismissed it as a curious, but inferior, imitation of *The Sacred Harp*.

The scholars William Tallmadge and Joe Dan Boyd, who were familiar with George Pullen Jackson's earlier work, made separate research trips to southeast Alabama in the late 1960s. Boyd's research resulted in a 1970 article in the *Journal of American Folklore* documenting the life of Judge Jackson and the publishing of *The Colored Sacred Harp*. In that same year, at Boyd's urging, a group of singers were invited to perform at the Smithsonian's Festival of American Folklife in Washington, D.C. The singers, mainly from Dale County, called themselves the Wiregrass Sacred Harp Singers. That festival appearance led to other engagements that continue today.

In 1950, Judge Jackson and a group of Dale County singers recorded, on 78 r.p.m. vinyl, two songs from *The Colored Sacred Harp*, both written by Jackson. "My Mother's Gone" was one of Jackson's earliest compositions commemorating the death of his mother. In the 1920s, Jackson had "My Mother's Gone" printed on broadsheets, which he gave and sold to friends and other singers. "Florida Storm," written by Jackson in 1928, commemorates the hurricane of 1926. Jackson's 1950 recording helped bring "My Mother's Gone" and "Florida Storm" to prominence in the community's active repertoire.

Not until the 1970s did there develop broader interest in preserving and promoting *The Colored Sacred Harp*. In 1973, the Wiregrass Sacred Harp

Singers arranged for a reprint of *The Colored Sacred Harp* with funding from the Alabama State Council on the Arts and the National Endowment for the Arts. Additional reprints followed in 1983 and 1992. Indeed, one of the basic intentions of the Wiregrass Sacred Harp singers was to promote *The Colored Sacred Harp*. In 1975, the Wiregrass Singers produced a long-playing record with selections from *The Colored Sacred Harp*, and in 1982, the Alabama State Council on the Arts in Montgomery produced the album *Wiregrass Notes: Black Sacred Harp Singing from Southeast Alabama*, on which four selections in a total of thirteen come from *The Colored Sacred Harp*. In 1993, ethnomusicologist Barbara Hampton traveled to Ozark, Alabama, for New World records, gathered together a group of seventeen singers, and recorded all seventy-seven songs in *The Colored Sacred Harp*. Fourteen of these songs were released on compact disc. In 1977, the American Folklife Center at the Library of Congress also recorded an album, *Yonder Come Day: Note Singing and Spirituals from South Georgia*, as part of its initiative in the South Central Georgia Wiregrass.

Marshall, " 'Keep on the Sunny Side of Life,' " is one of the first publications documenting the existence of bluegrass gospel. Marshall defines the form, 12–13. Bluegrass gospel music awaits full scholarly treatment. Neil Rosenberg in *Bluegrass: A History* (Urbana: University of Illinois Press, 1985) only touches upon it, 231–49.

In contrast, there has been a great deal of serious scholarship on the African American gospel tradition. Pearl William-Jones, "Afro-American Gospel Music: A Crystallization of the Black Aesthetic," *Ethnomusicology* 19 (1975): 373–385, has revealed a significant African influence in its distinctive performance styles and aesthetic requirements. On the basis of original ethnographic research in the field of sociolinguistics, Walter Pitts develops this theory further in *Old Ship of Zion: The Afro-Baptist Ritual in the African Diaspora* (New York: Oxford University Press, 1993). Wyatt Tee Walker in *"Somebody's Calling My Name": Black Sacred Music and Social Change* (Valley Forge, PA: Judson Press, 1979), gives an in-depth history of black gospel music. Michael Harris, *The Rise of Gospel Blues: The Music of Thomas Dorsey in the Urban Church* (New York: Oxford University Press, 1992), furnishes the first exhaustive biography of Thomas Dorsey. Harris overstates the urban appeal of black gospel music. Tommie Gabriel, an African American singer interviewed in Thomasville, Georgia, on March 23, 1994, reported a long history of traditional gospel performance in rural churches. Other singers whom I interviewed acknowledged having been influenced by the blues. On the role of the radio in transforming southern gospel music in general, see Cusic, *The Sound of Light*, 97. For a definitive treatment of the music, see Tony Heilbut's *The Gospel Sound* (New York:

Simon & Schuster, 1971) ("good news in"). Tommie Gabriel discussed one function of the music ("Maybe we can").

The quoted statement about the significance of the fifth Sunday comes from an interview with Gladys Westbrook, an African American Baptist, in Cairo, Georgia, on July 3, 1992 ("Congregation thought"). Most African American churches in the region still meet bimonthly. As a result, fifth Sundays are traditionally set aside for greater collective interaction. Singing conventions and Baptist district union meetings routinely convene on these weekends, so that fifth Sunday is a truly festive occasion.

Dave Stanley, "The Gospel-Singing Convention," 25, is among those making a link between specials and the quartet gospel music tradition. Karen Jackson, "The Royal Singing Convention," 504, also indicates that, by the 1920s, there was a general movement toward quartet group formation. Stanley Smith, the Alabama shape note singer, provided the quoted statement ("People like") during an interview in Ozark, Alabama, on June 9, 1994, and described the distinction that he makes between the two musical traditions. I have also quoted Charles Wolfe, "Gospel Goes Uptown: White Gospel Music, 1945–55," in *Folk Music and Modern Sound* (Jackson: University Press of Mississippi, 1982) ("under went in a").

William Jensen Reynolds in *A Joyful Sound: Christian Hymnody* (New York: Holt, Rinehart, & Winston, 1978), 104–105, explains the transition in the 1950s and 1960s from singing conventions to gospel sings. Don Cusic, *The Sound of Light*, apparently adopted Wolfe, "Gospel Goes Uptown," as a source on the all-night sing. Cusic, however, suggests (98) that all-night sings are obsolete. On the themes of southern gospel music, see Marshall's discussion of bluegrass gospel, " 'Keep on the Sunny Side of Life,' " 24–26. As the quoted statement about travel suggests ("must drive an"), the gospel music traditions sustain a network of enthusiasts who are constantly on the road.

6. Storytellers and Their Tales

Storytelling is one of the South's favorite forms of self-expression, as is evident from the scores of published anthologies and studies. Although few folktales have been collected from the Wiregrass, a start has recently been made. Mariella Hartsfield's *Tall Betsy and Dunce Baby: South Georgia Folktales* (Athens: University of Georgia Press, 1987) is holistic in its approach, and it provides the full context for the folk narratives it presents. Russell Reaver, Hartsfield's dissertation director, edited *Florida Folktales* (Gainesville: University of Florida Press, 1987). John Burrison's *Storytellers: Folktales and Legends of the South* (Athens: University of Georgia Press, 1989) also draws on actual field recordings rather than on material recycled from anthologies. Kay Cothran, one of Burrison's students, later published several important articles based on her own research. "Talking Trash in the Okefenokee Swamp Rim, Georgia" features a contextual analysis of Lem Griffis. It first appeared in the *Journal of American Folklore* 87 (1974): 340–56 and was reprinted in *Readings in American Folklore*, ed. Jan Brunvand (New York: Norton, 1979), 215–35. Elsie Surber's "A Study of the History and Folklore of the St. Andrews Bay Region" (master's thesis, University of Florida, 1950) contributed to our knowledge of another part of the Wiregrass, that is, the St. Andrews Bay region of Florida. Finally, hundreds of documents that were collected by the American Folklife Center— photographs, audiotapes, field notes, and transcripts—are housed at the Library of Congress.

Various works were helpful in defining the form of prose narrative under discussion: Kathryn Morgan's *Children of Strangers* (Philadelphia: Temple University Press, 1980) and Lynwood Montell's *Ghosts Along the Cumberland: Deathlore in the Kentucky Foothills* (Knoxville: University of Tennessee Press, 1975).

Some general works that discuss violence southern style include: Grady McWhiney, *Cracker Culture: The Celtic Ways in the Old South* (Tuscaloosa: University of Alabama Press, 1988), 146–70; William Lynwood Montell, *The Saga of Coe Ridge* (Knoxville: University of Tennessee Press, 1970); Pete Daniel, *Standing at the Crossroads: Southern Life Since 1900* (New York: Hill & Wang, 1986), 50–71; J. Wayne Flynt, *Poor but Proud: Alabama's Poor Whites* (Tuscaloosa: University of Alabama Press, 1989); Ted Ownby, *Subduing Satan: Religion, Recreation, and Manhood in the Rural South, 1865–1920* (Chapel Hill: University of North Carolina Press, 1990; Bertram Wyatt-Brown, *Southern Honor: Ethics and Behavior in the Old South* (New York: Oxford University Press, 1982). The statement regarding the southern propensity for violence is quoted from Raymond Gastil, *Cultural Regions of the United States* (Seattle: University of Washington Press, 1975), 185. See also Fred Watson, *Hub of the Wiregrass: A History of Houston County, Alabama, 1903–1972* (Anniston, AL: Higginbotham, 1972) ("Drunkenness, shootings"); 348, 355, on "tough towns" ("They would drink wild rum"); Val McGee, *Claybank Memories*, 203–204, on capital punishment as a solution to the violence ("Something must be"); and Flynt, *Poor but Proud*, 213, on white violence against blacks ("When poor").

About violent expectations I quote from Ida Belle Williams, *History of Tift County* (Macon, GA: J. W. Burke, 1948), 30–31 ("Native Georgians"), and "Swamp Gravy," a folk drama based on an oral history collection and periodically performed by residents of Colquitt, Georgia ("If you are"). Violence was often accepted as part of ordinary daily life within the region;

newspapers unabashedly reported the formation of posses and extralegal lynchings. Some writers reported violent episodes with nonchalance; I have quoted Fred Watson in *Hub of the Wiregrass*, 203 ("Leaving Dothan"). Another regional incident was documented in "The Camilla Massacre of 1868: Racial Violence as Political Propaganda," *Georgia History Quarterly* 71 (1987): 399–426. For the complete text of Fred Watson's statement ("On Dec. 3, 1864"), see *Piney Woods Echoes*, 185–86. Carswell's narrative statements ("I hate to") were made during an interview in Chipley, Florida, on May 6, 1994.

The quoted statement attributed to C. W. von Sydow comes from Lauri Honko's "Memorates and the Study of Folk Belief," *Journal of the Folklore Institute* 1 (1964): 5–18 ("Belief in the"). "The Ghost of Rit Hayes's Wife" appeared in Hartsfield, *Tall Betsy and Dunce Baby*, 62; the author is quoted from p. 55 ("Even in Grady"). Fred Smith, an African American whom I quote ("I woke up"), was interviewed in Cairo, Georgia, on June 29, 1994. Folklorist Richard Dorson annotates numerous references to both witch riding and cat witches in *Negro Folktales in Michigan* (Cambridge, MA: Harvard University Press, 1956), 221–23.

I collected the Bible stories about Moses from Tommie Gabriel ("So, he") during an interview in Thomasville, Georgia, on March 23, 1994, and from Doris Lewis ("The Lord taught") in Dothan, Alabama, on August 5, 1994. Zora Neale Hurston documented the propensity among African Americans to narrate traditional tales about Moses and his supernatural powers; see her *Mules and Men* (1935; reprint, Bloomington: Indiana University Press, 1963), 194, and her full-length fictional rendering, *Moses, Man of the Mountain* (1939; reprint, New York: Harper Perennial, 1991). See also Robert Hemenway's treatment of the motif in *Zora Neale Hurston: A Literary Biography* (Urbana: University of Illinois Press, 1977), 256–71. Lawrence Levine's *Black Culture, Black Consciousness* (New York: Oxford University Press, 1977) supplied the quoted statement (50) by a chaplain from the North soon after his arrival in Alabama in 1865 as well as other mentions of Moses in slave lore. Milton Young, an African American retired farmer in Graceville, Florida, furnished several memorates ("I liked") during an interview on June 24, 1994.

Connie Palmer, an American Indian folk artist, told me about the personal experience with the rattler at her door ("I called my husband") during an interview in Altha, Florida, on August 31, 1994. Folk singer Bessie Jones commented on the performance of the snake charmer in her memoirs ("He had some"), *For the Ancestors*, ed. John Stewart (Athens: University of Georgia Press, 1983), 26–27. The quotation of informant Ray Dominy ("They're becoming more prevalent") appeared in the field notes (90) of Dave Stanley from August 3, 1977, at the Library of Congress. Carswell discussed local snakes in *He Sold No 'Shine Before Its Time* (Chipley, FL: Williams, 1981), 32.

The buried treasure motif appears in various forms throughout the South, but Wiregrass Country seems to possess a special fondness for this type of tale. For instance, see Hartsfield, "Ghost Gives Pot of Gold," 61–62 and 130–31. Confederates were widely believed to have buried Confederate silver during the war. Richard Dorson has also reported the prevalence among African Americans in Michigan of tales involving buried treasure, 121–22. Also see Patrick Mullen, "The Folk Idea of Unlimited Good in American Buried Treasure Legends," *Journal of the Folklore Institute* 15 (1978): 209–20.

7. Games, Gatherings, and Special Occasions

For this chapter I consulted: Barbara Babcock, ed., *The Reversible World* (Ithaca, NY: Cornell University Press, 1978); Gregory Bateson, *Steps to an Ecology of Mind* (New York: Ballantine, 1972); Clifford Geertz, *The Interpretation of Cultures* (New York: Basic Books, 1973); Helen Schwartzman, *Transformations: The Anthropology of Children's Play* (New York: Plenum, 1978); Brian Sutton-Smith, "Games of Order and Disorder" (paper delivered at the symposium "Forms of Symbolic Inversion," American Anthropological Association, Toronto, Ontario, December 1, 1972); Brian Sutton-Smith, "Epilogue: Play as Performance," *Play and Learning* (New York: Gardner Press, 1979); Victor Turner, *The Ritual Process* (New York: Aldine, 1969).

J. Wayne Flynt astutely assesses the work cycle of the yeoman farmer in *Poor but Proud: Alabama's Poor Whites* (Tuscaloosa: University of Alabama Press, 1989), 212. Mariella Hartsfield, *Tall Betsy and Dunce Baby: South Georgia Folktales* (Athens: University of Georgia Press, 1987), also documented the balance that Wiregrass families established between work and play, 46.

See Frank Owsley, *Plain Folk of the Old South* (Baton Rouge: Louisiana State University Press, 1949), 90–132, for a generic portrayal of southern folklife. Flynt devotes a chapter to folklife in Wiregrass Alabama, in *Poor but Proud*, 211–42. I have quoted Georgia Griffin, *Ochlocknee: Land of Crooked Waters* (Thomasville, GA: Ochlocknee Community Civic Club, 1982), who suggests that things done best were done together and who describes pindar shellings, 182; and I quote J. L. Herring, *Saturday Night Sketches: Stories of Old Wiregrass Georgia* (Boston: Gorham, 1918), who gave a full account of these shellings, 169–74. E. W. Carswell, whom I have quoted, discussed "peanut-boiling season" in *Remembering Old Rhoady*

(Tallahassee, FL: Rose, 1993), 66. Herring also describes house-raisings and quilting bees, 268–71, and furnishes details about "cutting a bee tree," in *Saturday Night Sketches*, 147–51.

Quilting rituals have been widely reported. My sources included Elsie Surber, "A Study of the History and Folklore of the St. Andrews Bay Region" (M.A. thesis, University of Florida, 1950), 218. Fred Watson described the daily life of Wiregrass women in *Coffee Grounds* (Anniston, AL: Higginbotham, 1970), 28. African American quilting practices are described by Ophelia White.

Elsie Surber, "History and Folklore," speaks of extraordinary events in people's ordinary daily lives, 217. I have quoted Ted Ownby regarding the vigilance of the evangelicals; see *Subduing Satan: Religion, Recreation, and Manhood in the Rural South, 1865–1920* (Chapel Hill: University of North Carolina Press, 1990), 118. Arthur Powell highlights the subverting of religious restrictions in *I Can Go Home Again* (Chapel Hill: University of North Carolina Press, 1943), 93; as do Herring, *Saturday Night Sketches*, 255, and Surber, "History and Folklore," 224. Connie Palmer, who is of Creek descent, on August 31, 1994, in Altha, Florida, shared modern examples.

Dorothy Brannen in *Life in Old Bulloch: The Story of a Wiregrass County* (Gainesville, GA: Magnolia Press, 1987), 190–213, described how urbanization changed the prohibition against dancing. The popular tacky parties are mentioned in the *Cairo Messenger*, September 7, 1906.

On bay excursions I have quoted Surber, "History and Folklore," 218; Hartsfield, *Tall Betsy and Dunce Baby*, 58; and Carswell, *Old Rhoady*, 51. Fred Watson mentioned similar activities in Wiregrass Alabama in *Hub of the Wiregrass*, 90–91, and *Coffee Grounds*, 34.

"Oysters on the Half-Shell" appeared in Carswell's *Commotion in the Magnolia Tree* (Bonifay: Taylor, 1981), 28. Also, Georgia Griffin, *Ochlocknee*, 107, described oyster suppers as fund-raising events. Informant Bobby Roberts spoke of mullet season in an interview with folklorist Dave Stanley ("Mullet season is"), August 3, 1977; see Stanley's field notes, Library of Congress, 86. Carswell mentioned salt-cured mullet in *Commotion*, 29, and William Rogers, *Thomas County, 1865–1900* (Tallahassee: Florida State University Press, 1973), 250, mentioned fish wagons from the coast.

Hartsfield, in the appendix of *Tall Betsy and Dunce Baby*, provided narrative descriptions about the construction of the dumb-bull, 161–67. The foot-washing prank was reported in Griffin, *Ochlocknee*, 198. I learned of the goat prank from Maston O'Neal, *Prologue* (n.p.: author, 1985), 93. See also Rogers, *Thomas County*, about the weapons of young boys, 262. Carswell mentions his bow and arrows in *Old Rhoady*, 96. Brannen, *Life in Old Bulloch*, described the pushmobile scene, 420. Informant Ophelia White's reminiscence is from an interview in Sylvester, Georgia, on December 11, 1992.

For discussions of Southeastern Indian stickball, see Jesse Burt and Robert Ferguson, *Indians of the Southeast: Then and Now* (Nashville: Abingdon, 1973), 84–91, and William Winn, *The Old Beloved Path* (Eufaula, AL: Historic Chattahoochee Commission, 1992). The tradition of fireball lacks general documentation. The only reference located appeared in Joseph Oxendine's *American Indian Sports Heritage* (Champaign, IL: Human Kinetics Books, 1988), 63–64. Boysie McGriff, Connie Palmer, and Ophelia White (in separate interviews), however, remembered it. On townball and baseball, see Brannen ("The ball used" and "The colored"); see also Fred Watson, *Hub of the Wiregrass: A History of Houston County, Alabama, 1903–1972* (Anniston, AL: Higginbotham, 1972), 349 ("Pistols, billies").

For the quoted statements about Thanksgiving activities, see Brannen, *Life in Old Bulloch*, 485 ("Some went hunting"); and Ownby, *Subduing Satan*, 47 ("The traditional Southern"). About Christmas I have quoted Louise Westling, ed., *He Included Me: The Autobiography of Sarah Rice* (Athens: University of Georgia Press, 1989), 38 ("During Christmas season"); Surber, "History and Folklore," 222–23; I quote Brannen from *Bulloch Times* ("The population of"), 192; Ownby, *Subduing Satan*, 46 ("People too poor"); Helms, "Just Lookin' for a Home," 351; and E. W. Carswell, *Commotion in the Magnolia Tree* (Bonifay, FL: Taylor, 1982), 24–25 ("They never explained").

Far too many scholars mention Watch Night as being obsolete. They are generally unaware that African Americans continue to observe it. On January 1 as Emancipation Day I have quoted Rogers, *Thomas County*, 349 ("A Typical"). The rhyme ("Peas for peace") comes from an interview with Wallace Sholar, a grocer in Cairo, Georgia, on May 17, 1994. On New Year's, I have quoted Surber, "History and Folklore," 223 ("was supposed to").

Independence Day sketches appear in most of the county histories. I have quoted Herring, *Saturday Night Sketches*, 226–31 ("there was not"). Surber mentioned boat races in "History and Folklore," 220, and Griffin, *Ochlocknee* ("a pool hall"). I am grateful to several individuals who provided information about Emancipation Day celebrations within the Wiregrass: Boysie McGriff ("five barrels of"), Willie and Louise Johnson, Dewey Williams, Bertha and Owen Wrice ("one of the"), Tommie Gabriel, and Jack Hadley, an African American local historian. A monograph by William Wiggins combines an ethnographic look at contemporary celebrations with historical accounts: *O Freedom: Afro-American Emancipation Celebrations* (Knoxville: University of Tennessee Press, 1987). Also, see Wiggins's " 'Juneteenth': Afro-American Customs of the Emancipation," in

The Old Traditional Way of Life, ed. Robert Walls and George Schoemaker (Bloomington, IN: Trickster Press, 1989), 146–58. Jerry DeVine and Titus Brown, "The Twentieth of May: Celebrating African American Freedom South Georgia," *Journal of Southwest Georgia History* 8 (1993): 12–28, was very helpful ("Wednesday they would"). I have quoted Rogers, *Thomas County*, 348 ("In 1848 blacks"), on Emancipation Day.

Surber, "History and Folklore," 220 ("patriotic program held"), provides one of the only mentions of Decoration Day in Wiregrass Country. When I visited him within a week of this observance, E. W. Carswell mentioned that an association has formed to relocate the graves of Confederate soldiers in Washington County, Florida. Cemetery associations are common and sponsor routine cleanup and annual Decoration Days, often with entertainment. Notices of cemetery fund-raising drives and columns soliciting funds appear regularly in local newspapers. An article by Lynwood Montell discusses the significance of these customs in "Cemetery Decoration Customs in the American South," in *The Old Traditional Way of Life*, 111–29. Bessie Jones is quoted about graveyard decorations ("People decorated") from *For the Ancestors*, ed. John Stewart (Athens: University of Georgia Press, 1983), 76. Boysie McGriff spoke of African American funerary customs in an interview ("seven days of"). John Vlach, *The Afro-American Tradition in Decorative Arts* (Cleveland: Cleveland Museum of Art, 1978), 139, furnished the other quoted statement, followed by Tommie Gabriel's comment ("Here's an illustration").

Charivari, a custom relating to the need of a community to maintain the social order, is discussed in relation to lynch laws in Bertram Wyatt-Brown, *Southern Honor: Ethics and Behavior in the Old South* (New York: Oxford University Press, 1982). I have quoted Surber, "History and Folklore," 215–16 ("In front rode" and "The 'Shivaree' "). The quotation regarding the wedding dinner comes from *Collections of Early County Historical Society* (n.p., 1971), 112 ("I must digress"); see also Brannen, *Life in Old Bulloch*, 38 ("Here was gathered"). Herring, *Saturday Night Sketches*, 39–41, provided a sketch of "running up the groom." See Rogers, *Thomas County*, 318, on the cakewalk in Thomasville, Georgia.

8. Festivals and Other Public Events

Ideas for this chapter were informed by the following works: Roger Abrahams, "The Language of Festivals: Celebrating the Economy," in *Celebration* (Washington, DC: Smithsonian Institution Press, 1982); Mikhail Bakhtin, *Rabelais and His World*, trans. Helen Iswolsky (1965; reprint, Bloomington: Indiana University Press, 1984); Allessandro Falassi, *Time*

Out of Time (Albuquerque: University of New Mexico Press, 1987); Bob Janiskee, "South Carolina's Harvest Festivals: Rural Delights for Day Tripping Urbanites," *Journal of Cultural Geography* 1 (1980): 96–104; Bob Janiskee, "Rural Festivals in South Carolina," *Journal of Cultural Geography* 11 (1991): 31–41; Beverly Stoeltje, "Festival in America," in *Handbook of American Folklore*, ed. Richard Dorson (Bloomington: Indiana University Press, 1983); Beverly Stoeltje and Richard Bauman, "Community Festival and the Enactment of Modernity," in *The Old Traditional Way of Life*, ed. Robert Walls and George Schoemaker (Bloomington: Trickster Press, 1989); and Victor Turner, *Dramas, Fields, and Metaphors: Symbolic Action in Human Society* (Ithaca, NY: Cornell University Press, 1974).

In Wiregrass Country, the festival season generally wanes during the dog days of summer but picks up again with the Labor Day weekend and continues through April.

The mayhaw has generally escaped commentary because it grows within a very limited area even within the Wiregrass. About mayhaws I have quoted Arthur Powell, *I Can Go Home Again* (Chapel Hill: University of North Carolina Press, 1943), 56 ("It is made"). See also E. W. Carswell's reminiscence in *Commotion in the Magnolia Tree* (Bonifay, FL: Taylor, 1982), 30. Other details about mayhaw jelly come from interviews with Ophelia White ("There was some" and "Mayhaws"), Betty Wrice, Katie Potts, Joy Jenks, and Pearly Broome.

E. W. Carswell, *He Sold No 'Shine Before Its Time* (Chipley, FL: Williams, 1981), 35, describes the possum hunt. On the importance of the mule, see William Ferris, *You Live and Learn. Then You Die and Forget It All: Ray Lum's Tales of Horses, Mules and Men* (New York: Doubleday, 1992). E. W. Carswell dedicated his book *Remembering Old Rhoady* (Tallahassee, FL: Rose, 1993), to the family mule; I have quoted him from p. 102 ("indebted to" and "was mischievous").

On family caning I have quoted Marilyn Barrett Connell of the William Henry Faircloth Family, as stated in *Gleanings: A Community's Memories of People at the Crossroads of a Place*, ed. Wessie Connell et al. (Cairo, GA: Roddenberry Library, 1987), 78 ("They would"). For the suggestion that moonshine was a form of social security, see the field notes of Dave Stanley, 13, for July 16, 1977 ("a woman who"), Library of Congress. Carswell supplied moonshining information in his title piece, *He Sold No 'Shine*, 19 ("Silas was a"). Ophelia White furnished the extended narrative describing the production of cane buck in an interview in Sylvester, Georgia, on December 11, 1992 ("As I told"). Owen Wrice spoke of the abundance of cane syrup in an interview in Quitman, Georgia, on June 16, 1994 ("would grind out"); on drinking cane and the saying I have quoted *Gleaning*, 198–99 ("I recall my"). Carswell spoke of cane as hog fodder in *Remembering Old Rhoady*, 103 ("my father who").

Olin Pope ("I wish that") lamented his inability to acquire fresh meats in an interview. Ophelia White described in an interview how her grandfather prepared sausage ("My grandfather knew"). Additional reminiscences came from Olin Pope and Owen Wrice ("we take that"). Richardson's Barb-B-Que was discussed in interviews with Delia Richardson and Edward Weatherspoon ("We had airplanes") in Iron City, Georgia, on June 29, 1994.

Folks Huxford described firemen's musters and the activities associated with firefighters in *The History of Brooks County Georgia* (Homersville, GA: author, 1949), 183 ("These Negro"). On county fairs throughout the region, see Dorothy Brannen's account in *Life in Old Bulloch: The Story of a Wiregrass County* (Gainesville, GA: Magnolia Press, 1987), 412.

Beauty pageants appear to be at their height. Women of the baby boomer generation recall contests to choose a homecoming queen, but now the pageants begin with babies and include men in "king" contests. The only folkloristic work on the subject to date is Robert Lavenda, "Minnesota Queen Pageants: Play, Fun, and Dead Seriousness in a Festival Mode," *Journal of American Folklore* 101 (1988): 168–75. See also Stoeltje and Bauman, "Community Festival."

Folklorists generally have also neglected football games. The most notable qualitative research on the subject is that done by David Snow et al., "Football Victory Celebrations in America," *Symbolic Interaction* 4 (1981): 101–16. High School football coach Ralph Jones was interviewed in Cairo, Georgia, on June 6, 1994 ("Everybody has something").

9. Outdoor Activities

Works on hunting and fishing in the South include: Grady McWhiney, *Cracker Culture* (Tuscaloosa: University of Alabama Press, 1988), 138–45; Ted Ownby, *Subduing Satan: Religion, Recreation, and Manhood in the Rural South, 1865–1920* (Chapel Hill: University of North Carolina Press, 1990); Terry Jordan and Matti Kaups, *The American Backwoods Frontier* (Baltimore: Johns Hopkins University Press, 1989).

Dave Mathis is quoted from Dave Stanley's interview on August 19, 1977, as it appears in his field notes, 208 ("The best time"), for the South Central Georgia Folklife Project at the Library of Congress.

I have quoted from William Rogers's "A Land for Sportsmen," in *Thomas County, 1865–1900* (Tallahassee: Florida State University Press, 1973), 247 ("Expeditions combining"). Fieldworker Thomas Adler of the

South Central Georgia Folklife Project collected this statement on August 18, 1977; see Tape No. GA7-TA-R22, at the Library of Congress ("The men would go").

J. L. Herring provided the descriptive statement that I have quoted about fire hunts, in *Saturday Night Sketches: Stories of Old Wiregrass Georgia* (Boston: Gorham, 1918), 237 ("The boys had"). E. W. Carswell has provided a regional update on these hunting practices under "Hunting and Fishing," in *He Sold No 'Shine Before Its Time* (Chipley, FL: Williams, 1981), 33–42. For the commentary on crow hunting, see "Hunters Usually Eat Crow," 34–35 in the same volume ("Crows seem to").

The term "snipe hunting" refers not to the bird but to a prank played on outsiders and young initiates to the sport. Dave Stanley's account appears in an interview with Bobby Roberts, field notes, 87, on August 3, 1977 ("Roberts asked if").

The dove shoot is second only to quail hunting in the region. See Georgia Griffin, *Ochlocknee: Land of Crooked Water* (Thomasville, GA: Ochlocknee Community Civic Club, 1982), 179. For another discussion of the sport, see Rogers, *Thomas County*, 261. Ownby, *Subduing Satan*, 28, spoke of the baiting of fields to attract the more wary game birds ("True sportsmen").

Tad Tuleja, "The Turkey," *American Wildlife in Symbol and Story* (Knoxville: University of Tennessee Press, 1987), 26 ("Turkey hunting"), offers a full treatment of this bird. Dave Stanley recaps the tall tale in his field notes from an interview with informant Raymond Green, 237–38, August 21, 1977 ("Uncle Sam went"). Fred Watson describes a typical turkey shoot in *Coffee Grounds* (Anniston, AL: Higginbotham, 1970), 28. See also Charles Elliott, *Ichauway Plantation* (n.p.: Robert Woodruff, 1974), 55–61. Ted Ownby, *Subduing Satan*, discusses in great detail the tendency of some hunters to kill game wantonly by devious means, 32.

The quail has a significant place in the Wiregrass ecological system and may have a wide range of symbolic meanings, especially with regard to its slaughter and preservation. It is also noteworthy that outsiders from the North gave the bird its status as game. Rogers, *Thomas County*, describes its significance in Thomas County, perhaps the center of these hunting plantations in the South, 259–60 ("The sports"). He includes some of the folk beliefs about quails. H. L. Beadel, "Fire Impressions," in *Proceedings, Tall Timbers Fire Ecology Conference*, Tallahassee, Florida, March 1–2, 1962, 4, describes the ritual closing of the season on hunting plantations ("on the last"). Willie and Louise Johnson, Tommie Gabriel ("father came back"), and Jack Hadley were indispensable and furnished oral histories about their experiences growing up on these hunting plantations.

Hunters are bound to develop close attachments with their hunting dogs.

Ownby, *Subduing Satan,* commented on their significance ("Though many could"), 21. William Rogers, *Thomas County,* 247, speaks of their death as an emotional loss ("It is doubtful"). They also contributed to the expressive lying common in the region. Dave Stanley's field notes of August 12, 1977, recorded at the home of Luther A. Bailey, sometimes known as "Lying" Bailey, furnish one example ("You talking about"). Kay Cothran, "Talking Trash in the Okefenokee Swamp Rim, Georgia," in John Burrison's *Story-tellers: Folktales and Legends of the South* (Athens: University of Georgia Press, 1989), 118, features the tall tales of Lem Griffis ("What about dogs?"). Also, E. W. Carswell, *Remembering Old Rhoady,* supplied several quoted statements ("That sly fox" and "I like to," 27 and 110, respectively). Another quoted comment comes from an interview with Carolyn Chason in Cairo, Georgia, on May 25, 1994 ("My father would"). I have quoted Ownby, *Subduing Satan,* 24–28, on hunting as an act of manly achievement.

The tall tale and joke about unbelievable catches are quoted from Dave Stanley's field notes of August 3, 1977, from an interview with informant J. C. Cooper, 114 ("one man says"). Carswell mentions his folk belief about fishing in *He Sold No 'Shine,* 39 ("The 'beds' "). Informant C. L. Talley reported other folk beliefs in an interview with Dave Stanley on July 20, 1977, 38 ("Go cat fishing"), and were recorded by Stanley in Aaron's Barbershop in Fitzgerald, 93. Rogers, *Thomas County,* also comments on fishing traditions, 248–49 ("Thomas countians"), and the fishing ditty ("When de win's"). Ophelia White provided the quote about "mudding" ("I know what") and her love of the sport ("I love fishing"). Ownby, *Subduing Satan,* 34, reported the underhanded method of enhancing one's catch. Dave Stanley's field notes describe another method, 128 ("Mr. Rice mentioned"). Stanley also recorded in his field notes, 66, for July 26, 1977, that wiregrass was actually used to capture worms ("[Chuck Royal]"). Stanley's field notes, 88, for August 3, 1977, also provide the best description of grunting worms ("You use").

On yardscapes I consulted Mark Francis and Randolph Hester, Jr., eds., *The Meaning of Gardens: Ideas, Place, and Action* (Cambridge, MA: MIT Press, 1990); Gray Gundaker, "Tradition and Innovations in African-American Yards," *African Arts* 26 (1993): 58–96. John Hunt and Joachim Wolschke-Bulmahn, eds., *The Vernacular Garden* (Washington, DC: Dumbarton Oaks Research Library and Collection, 1993); Mara Miller, *The Garden as Art* (Albany: State University of New York Press, 1993); John Vlach, *The Afro-American Tradition in Decorative Arts* (Cleveland: Cleveland Museum of Art, 1978); and Richard Westmacott, *African-American Gardens and Yards* (Knoxville: University of Tennessee Press, 1992).

Richard Westmacott fails to differentiate between gardens and yards. He tends to use the terms interchangeably in *African American Gardens and Yards in the Rural South* (Knoxville: University of Tennessee Press, 1992). Although he initially distinguished between them, he observed, "In this study the term garden is sometimes used broadly to cover all these areas," 22. I suggest that a broader term, "yardscape," is required to denote this range of open space.

See Alice Walker, *In Search of Our Mothers' Gardens* (New York: Harcourt Brace Jovanovich, 1983), 241. Miller, *The Garden as Art*, supplied the definition of garden, 98 ("Gardens are not"). I take exception, however, with Paul Gloth, "Parking Gardens," in *The Meaning of Gardens*. Gloth uses the term "yard" to mean an enclosure that does not "imply human presence or upkeep," 131. In regions like Wiregrass Country, yards are spaces that necessarily involve both. Yards afford utilitarian space for gatherings; neglect of yards, moreover, creates possible danger. For African Americans, in particular, the swept yard was traditionally both a social space and a safe space. Given the prevalence of snakes in the region, yards are consciously maintained for use. On the informal garden I have quoted Miller, *The Garden as Art*, 22.

I have quoted Kathleen Condon from " 'Learnin', Though' ": Environmental Art as a Creative Process," in *Arts in Earnest: North Carolina Folklife* (Durham: Duke University Press, 1990), 191. Charles Lewis, "Gardens as Healing Process," in *The Meaning of Gardens*, 245 ("The power"). Some of the yardscape artists consulted include: Katie Potts of Troy, Alabama; Lizzie Henry of Tifton, Georgia; Gladys Westbrook of Cairo, Georgia; Mrs. Poole of Thomasville, Georgia; Betty MacDougal-Daffin of Valdosta, Georgia; and Doris Lewis of Dothan, Alabama.